PLAYS OF
THE PIONEERS

PLAYS OF
THE PIONEERS

A BOOK OF HISTORICAL
PAGEANT–PLAYS

BY

CONSTANCE D'ARCY MACKAY

One-Act Play Reprint Series

 Core Collection Books, inc.

GREAT NECK, NEW YORK

First Published 1915
Reprinted 1976

International Standard Book Number
0-8486-2005-4

Library of Congress Catalog Number
76-40389

PRINTED IN THE UNITED STATES OF AMERICA

CONTENTS

PREFACE

ALL over the country, in normal schools and teachers' training-schools, in colleges, in village and city dramatic clubs, and in the junior and senior years of the high schools there is a growing development of the festival spirit—a spirit that desires something that can be given easily, that has opportunities for simple, colorful costumes and dances; that does not require as strenuous rehearsing as a long play, and that is dependent on its picturesqueness rather than on any sweeping dramatic climax which demands professional art from amateur players. To fill such needs this volume is intended. It gives full directions for music that is readily obtainable, and for costumes and scene setting, as well as a bibliography and notes on the plays.

Almost all the plays have already been acted as single episodes in pageants written and staged by the author. It needed but little changing to make them adaptable for all parts of the country. They deal, through history and symbol, with varying aspects of the pioneer spirit North, South, East, West, whose totality of effort has resulted in the making of America.

PLAYS OF THE PIONEERS

The following play forms the lyric interlude in the Pageant of Pioneers now in rehearsal in some of the smaller farming communities of the Dakotas and other Western states. This pageant is not a pageant of a given place, but of a movement — the Pioneer Movement — with episodes adaptable and applicable to any locality that has witnessed the coming of the pioneers, their vicissitudes, and final triumphs.

The drama-vitalization of the farming community—if it may so be called—which is being fostered by the admirable Little Country Theater of the North Dakota Agricultural College and by such periodicals as *The Farmer's Wife*, is bringing a new note of recreation into farm life, and filling the play-hours of the community with imaginative and co-operative pleasure.

PLAYS OF THE PIONEERS

THE PIONEERS

CHARACTERS:

THE PIONEER MAN   THE GRAY AND BROWN ONES
THE PIONEER WOMAN   OF THE FOREST
THE POWERS OF THE FOREST   FEVER
THE SPIRIT OF THE WILDERNESS   FAMINE
THE POWERS OF THE RIVER   DEATH
THE MIST MAIDENS

The scene is a natural clearing in the primeval forest, with trees right, left, and background.

At the sound of a clear bird note, THE SPIRIT OF THE WILDERNESS, *in flowing garments of lichen-gray with touches of earth-brown and leaf-green, enters from left, and beckons forth* THE POWERS OF THE FOREST, *who enter from left, looking like sylvan goddesses in draperies of leaf-green and darker pine-green. They come lightly onto the stage to Dvorak's "Hu-*

moresque." They dance swayingly at right, left, and background, with motions that suggest the tossing of trees. As the "Humoresque" ends, THE SPIRIT OF THE WILDERNESS goes fleetly to background, and beckons to THE POWERS OF THE RIVER, who sweep in to the bright strains of the "Pizzicato" from the ballet "Sylvia." They are clad in deep and pale blues, like the deeps and shallows of water. Their dance with THE POWERS OF THE FOREST expresses all the untrammeled joy of untamed creatures. They in turn, as their dance with THE POWERS OF THE FOREST ends, summon by entreating gestures THE MIST MAIDENS, who dwell near the river in background. At their summons THE MIST MAIDENS enter from background, robed in filmy white, with crowns of water-lilies on their hair. Their entrance music is MacDowell's "To a Water-lily," and they dance with THE POWERS OF THE FOREST and THE POWERS OF THE RIVER as lightly and weavingly as mist stealing across a meadow. Just as the dance is ending there is a shot at left. For a moment the dancers pause, as if sculptured in stone. Then THE POWERS OF THE RIVER and THE MIST MAIDENS flee to background and exeunt. THE POWERS OF THE FOREST exeunt right, and pause a moment ere they disappear, *while* THE SPIRIT OF THE WILDERNESS, *who is the last to go, pauses with them, and stands for a moment ere she exits with a look of anger graven on her face, as if she would see who dared to break into her kingdom. A few notes of menace and foreboding are sounded as she withdraws.*

At the edge of the woods, left, down stage, THE PIONEER MAN *and* THE PIONEER WOMAN *enter, wearing Puritan garb, the man in black, with a black cloak, the woman in deep, bright blue, with a blue cloak and a white cap and kerchief. Her dress is splotched with mud and torn with briers. The man carries a pack and gun. The woman carries a bundle. Both* THE PIONEER MAN *and* THE PIONEER WOMAN *are young and fearless-looking. As they step out of the woods two Indian arrows fly through the air from left. The* WOMAN *draws closer to her husband. They pause a moment, arrested in their progress, tense, expectant,* THE PIONEER MAN *with his hand on his gun,* THE PIONEER WOMAN *controlled and quiet, though with a look of terror on her face. There is no further sign of hostility, and with the aspect of those who draw a deep breath of relief,* THE PIONEER MAN *and* THE PIONEER WOMAN *come slowly forward.*

PLAYS OF THE PIONEERS

The Pioneer Man

With sun to scorch, and rain to chill,
The Powers of the Forest,
The Powers of the River
Menace us always:
The Unseen Terror lurketh around us.

> [*Indicates arrows.*]

Wilt thou go forward?

The Pioneer Woman

Where thou goest, I go.
The rains shall not daunt me,
Nor the heat slay me.
I fare where thou farest.
That which we face we shall conquer at length.

> [*They set resolutely forward. But
> at their first step* The Spirit of the
> Wilderness, *followed by all* The
> Powers of the Forest, *suddenly
> bears down upon them, to the music
> of "The Hall of the Mountain
> King," from the "Peer Gynt" Suite,
> by Grieg.* The Powers of the
> Forest *are no longer light and play-*

[14]

ful in their aspect. They sweep forward, with tree-branches, oak, maple, and pine in their hands with which they lash out at THE PIONEER *and his wife. Among* THE POWERS OF THE FOREST *now are seen two grayish-black and two brownish-clad figures, with animal heads, pricked ears, and bright eyes. These also fly at the man and his wife as if they would tear them to bits. Their gestures are ravening, like the claw of the panther-cat.* THE PIONEER MAN *puts his arm up to shield his face, pressing forward a step at a time, his wife behind him.*]

THE PIONEER MAN

The Powers of the Forest
Battle against us!

THE PIONEER WOMAN

Thine be the victory!
We shall press forward!

[THE SPIRIT OF THE WILDERNESS *and* THE POWERS OF THE FOREST *give way before* THE PIONEER, *and exeunt with dark looks, right. As they go, up from the background stream* THE POWERS OF THE RIVER, *still to the skirl of "The Hall of the Mountain King," with white scarfs in their hands representing foam. They lash out at* THE PIONEER MAN *and his wife menacingly.*]

THE PIONEER MAN

The Powers of the River
Battle against us!

THE PIONEER WOMAN

Thy strong arm shall conquer!
Forward! I follow!

[*He pushes forward, and* THE POWERS OF THE RIVER *give way, and exeunt, background.*]

Now rest thee a moment.

[*Somewhat wearily the man follows the woman to center foreground,*

where they sit, and THE PIONEER
MAN *kindles a fire, and swings a
kettle from out of his pack, the
woman helping him.*]

THE PIONEER MAN

How shall it be with thee
Here in the wilderness?
Thou who hast woven
Safe by the hearthside,
Thou who hast culled
Flowers from sweet gardens
Sun-warmed and sheltered.
How will it be with thee
Here in the wilderness?

THE PIONEER WOMAN [*bravely*]

I will weave furs and fiber for clothing,
Herbs of the fields I will have
For my garden,
Soothing and healing.
Now rest thee, oh, rest thee,
Here for a moment where naught is to fear.

[THE PIONEER MAN *rests and drowses
by the fire, while his wife rises, gathers*

some herbs near by, and puts them in kettle. Then she wanders farther, right, stooping and culling. As soon as her back is turned THE MIST MAIDENS *steal in from background to the strains of "Anitra's Dance," from the "Peer Gynt" Suite, played softly at first, and then louder. They weave a dance about* THE PIONEER MAN, *and exeunt toward background as his wife sees them and hurries to foreground. At her touch on his shoulder* THE PIONEER MAN *still drowses, as if overcome with stupor.*]

THE PIONEER WOMAN

The touch of long fingers,
Shadowy, tenuous,
Boding of evil!
Rouse thee, my husband!
Mists from the rivers,
Mists from the swamp-lands,
Rising and stealing
The life from our pulses!
Rouse thee!
Oh, rouse thee!

THE PIONEERS

[*From left, while* THE PIONEER
WOMAN *speaks,* FEVER *approaches,
a tall feminine figure in scarlet
draperies, with a scarlet veil bound
about her brows and flowing hair.
Her face is colorless, her eyes blaz-
ingly bright, her lips deep carmine.
She enters to the second movement of
"Anitra's Dance," and stands above*
THE PIONEER MAN *with gestures of
mocking incantation as* THE PIONEER
WOMAN *fills a cup from the herb brew
in the kettle and presses it to the
man's lips.*]

FEVER

Nay, ere thou risest
Reckon with me!
I am the Fever.
In vain thou dost wrestle.
Poison my touch is.
Fire my caresses.

[*She bends over him lightly.*]

Thou shalt not escape me!
I am the figure
Born of delirium!

THE PIONEER WOMAN [*agonized*]

Drink, I beseech thee!
Drink!

    FEVER [*tauntingly*]

Put thy hot hand
To the cup that she holdeth.

> [THE PIONEER MAN *takes the cup.*
> *His hand shakes as he holds it. His*
> *wife places her hand over his to steady*
> *it, and guides the cup to his lips.*]

    THE PIONEER WOMAN

Drink. I am here.
Do not fear.
I am near thee.
The Fever shall leave thee at touch of these herbs.

> [*As he drinks, exit* FEVER, *right.*
> THE PIONEER MAN *closes his eyes*
> *for a moment, then opens them, smil-*
> *ing, with renewed vigor, and bends to*
> *assist his wife to rise. She looks*
> *even more pale and spent than he.*
> *As he bends to her,* FAMINE, *clad in*

[20]

dull gray, with pale face and dark-circled eyes, enters from left to the opening bars of " The Death of Ase," from the same suite.]

FAMINE

Fever shall leave thee.
Yea, but thou reckonest
Hereafter with me.

[FAMINE *raises her arms triumphantly.* THE PIONEER MAN *rises, holding his wife, and strives to repulse* FAMINE.]

I am the Famine,
The breath of the places
Where creatures are wary
And come not to traps.
I am ill-fortune in hunting and fishing.

[THE PIONEER MAN *tries to raise his gun, but is too weak. His wife droops by the fire, unable to cope with* FAMINE.]

I weaken thy wrist,
And thy aim is unsteady.

PLAYS OF THE PIONEERS

The fishes I draw
From the pools and the rivers;
They come not for all of thy craft and thy patience.
Drought is my gift to thee;
Rains that send rotting
The seed that thou plantest.
I am all nature arming against thee!

[*Yet* THE PIONEER MAN *presses forward, and* FAMINE *withdraws, left, as* THE PIONEER *tears roots from the ground and finds a few berries. With these he goes back to his wife.*]

THE PIONEER MAN

See, I have brought thee
Berries and roots.
Look up, and take heart!
We shall conquer the Famine.
Eat.

THE PIONEER WOMAN

Thou art starving thyself of thy portion!

THE PIONEERS

The Pioneer Man

Lean thou on me.
We still shall press forward.

> [*As the woman rises he sweeps together their merchandise, and the woman leans against him, supported by his arm, as out of the woods at left, unseen by them, comes* DEATH, *a sinister male figure all in black, over which a white skeleton is outlined. His head is a grinning skeleton mask.*]

DEATH [*with hollow menace*]

Fool! In the dark,
In the sunlight, I follow!
I lurk near thy footsteps
Wherever thou goest.
Reckon with me!

The Pioneer Man [*aghast*]
Death!

> [*He holds his wife closer to him.*]

DEATH [*with power and triumph*]
Death!
Thou hast named me!

[23]

Thee I shall conquer,
Quenching thy will.
All dreams and ambitions,
All hoping and struggle,
End as I conquer.

[*As* DEATH *and* THE PIONEER MAN *grapple, hand to hand,* THE PIONEER WOMAN *falls to her knees. Three times* DEATH *and* THE PIONEER MAN *wrestle, and the third time* DEATH *is overcome and exits, left, leaving* THE PIONEER MAN *triumphant.*]

THE PIONEER WOMAN

Forward! Press forward!
Death thou hast conquered!

[*As* DEATH *exits, right, down stage,* THE SPIRIT OF THE WILDERNESS *appears at right, up stage; but a great change has taken place in her demeanor. On her wild hair rests a crown of roses; over her shoulder floats the purple cloak of victory. As* THE PIONEER MAN *and his wife*

THE PIONEERS

*gaze at her she approaches a step or
two, benignly, her hands outstretched,
and holding a laurel wreath.*]

THE WILDERNESS SPIRIT

Victory! Victory!
Thine at the last!
The Wilderness Spirit
Stand I before thee,
Tamed by thy courage.

> [*As* THE SPIRIT OF THE WILDER-
> NESS *speaks* THE POWERS OF THE
> FOREST *steal out humbly, and the
> branches that a little while since were
> used to impede the progress of* THE
> PIONEER MAN *and his wife are now
> laid at their feet. The brown and
> gray creatures of the forest put down
> fur, then withdraw warily and stand
> back of* THE POWERS OF THE FOR-
> EST. *From background come* THE
> POWERS OF THE RIVER. *They bring
> a bark bowl filled with water, which
> they deposit at the feet of* THE
> PIONEERS, *with supplicating ges-
> tures. While these are entering,* THE

PLAYS OF THE PIONEERS

Spirit of the Wilderness *continues speaking, indicating the different groups as they approach.*]

The Powers of the Forest,
The Powers of the River
Ye shall subdue.
They shall be to ye
Fire for the winter,
Shelter and roof-tree,
Skins for thy covering.

[*Indicates* The Powers of the
River.]

And for thy harvests
Moisture abundant.

[*As* The Pioneer Man *and his wife
stand up stage for a moment ere they
exeunt, left,* The Powers of the
Forest *and* The Powers of the
River *break into song and, with
gestures indicating their humbleness
and willingness to serve, follow the
man and his wife into the forest,
where the sound of an ax breaking
through the song indicates that* The

THE PIONEERS

PIONEERS *are beginning to build*
their wilderness home.]

SONG

[*To the "Melody in F" by Rubinstein*]

To thee be victory, oh Pioneers!
  Danger encircled by day and night.
Here light thy hearth-fire to gleam through the
    years
  Clear as a beacon light.

Powers of the Forest and Powers of the River
  Here shall obey thee, working thy will.
Pine boughs that whisper, aspens that quiver,
  Sing to thee, "Conquer still!"

THE FOUNTAIN OF YOUTH
A FANTASY

THE FOUNTAIN OF YOUTH

A FANTASY

CHARACTERS:

THE GUARDIAN OF THE FOUNTAIN   PONCE DE LEON
A DAUGHTER OF THE DAWN   SILVA
OTHER DAUGHTERS OF THE DAWN   CORDOBA   } His followers

PLACE—*Florida.*

TIME—*The spring of 1523.*

SCENE—*A clearing in a forest wrought by nature, not by man. Trees right, left, and background, with deep ferns and forest tangle amidst the tree-trunks. Moss and vines swing from the branches of the trees.*

    Enter from the right, to the strains of Mendelssohn's "Spring Song," the DAUGHTERS OF THE DAWN, *clad in Neo-Grecian robes of pale and deep pink, the varying shades of dawn color. They are shod with pink sandals. Their hair falls about their shoulders. Their dance*

[31]

resembles a dance of the hours. *As it ends they turn toward right with gestures of obeisance, and presently from right enters* THE GUARDIAN OF THE FOUNTAIN, *robed in white, with silver sandals, and the Morning Star caught in her hair. She holds aloft, as one would hold a grail, a crystal cup in which sparkles water from the Fountain of Youth. Instantly she becomes the center of a dance of worship, to the strains of Lack's "Idyllo." Throughout the dance she holds the mystic cup within her hands, and toward the end of the dance turns again to right, and exits, followed by the* DAUGHTERS OF THE DAWN.

As they exeunt, from left appear PONCE DE LEON, SILVA, *and* CORDOBA. *Their clothing, once splendid, is now worn and stained with travel.* PONCE DE LEON, *in dull crimson, is a man of middle age, with noble bearing and a questing look.* SILVA, *with rusty cuirass and dark-green cloak, is younger, and discouraged-looking.* CORDOBA *is old and rugged, with white hair and the look of a mariner. His costume is midnight blue. There are huge gold rings in his ears.*

PONCE DE LEON [1]

I thought that I heard music! 'Twas a dream.

[1] The English pronunciation of the name is used.

THE FOUNTAIN OF YOUTH

Cordoba

A dream wrought of fatigue and endless search:
I pray thee let us rest us here a little.
I followed thee from Spain to Porto Rico,
Across strange seas, guided by unknown stars,
But never on such bitter quest as this.

Ponce de Leon

To find the Fountain of immortal Youth—
Ye call *that* bitter? All our nights and days
Of weariness shall be a story told
When once we taste of it.

Cordoba

              Oh, Ponce de Leon,
I would that we were back in sunny Spain!

> [Cordoba *and* Silva *sit on fallen
> tree-trunk, left foreground.* Cordo-
> ba *drinks from a leather flask and
> passes it to* Silva. *As these two talk*
> Ponce de Leon *looks raptly before
> him.*]

Silva

And half a league behind us there lie men

3   [33]

Outwearied in a search for what has proved
A hope like fool's fire, leading on and on.

PONCE DE LEON

So said ye when I sought the Western Ind,
But this— Ah, this! Dost thou remember it,
The golden day when first we heard of it?
And an old mariner with sea-bright eyes
And bronzèd face all scarred with ocean storms
Whispered that in the new Americas
Bubbled a fountain crystal clear, whose taste
Was nectar of the gods: and, like the gods,
Whoso should taste of it should ne'er grow old.
And is it strange that this, the youngest land,
Should hold Youth's Fountain? Count us for-
   tunate
That we are bound on such a mighty quest.

CORDOBA [*with utter weariness*]

Fortunate!

PONCE DE LEON

          Have not all things smiled on us?
Did we not find this land on Easter day?
A blessed omen! And I christened it
Florida. Flower of Easter!

THE FOUNTAIN OF YOUTH

SILVA [*darkly*]

                    What of thorns?
Hunger, fatigue, stark thirst, and aching limbs?

PONCE DE LEON

Why, look ye, if I find that fountain-head
There'll be no age, nor any grief, nor pain;
Only immortal Youth for all the world.
Others have sought for riches or for lands,
Or honor for their sovereigns, rank, and fame.
But I seek Youth, the lodestar of mankind—
Yea, what are all discoveries to this:—
To keep the thrill and rapture of life's dawn,
Feet that outrun the winds, adventurous hearts
All unencompassed by the chill of age;
To know this flesh will ne'er be witherèd,
Nor this strong arm weakened by passing years.
Go back to where the camp-fire shines for ye,
For this is my adventure. Leave me here.
I will rejoin ye later in the day.
Farewell.

CORDOBA [*to* SILVA, *who is half reluctant*]

          Come, Silva, let us leave him here.

               [PONCE DE LEON *stands with his*
               back to them, searching with eagle

glance the country before him. Cordoba *and* Silva, *with a backward
glance or two, exeunt, left. As
soon as* Ponce de Leon *feels that
they are gone he strides abruptly forward. As he nears the spot where
the fountain is concealed the* Daughters of the Dawn, *led by one of
their number, suddenly appear, to bar
his passage. For an instant, as he
were dreaming,* Ponce de Leon
brushes his hand across his eyes.]

A Daughter of the Dawn

Beware, rash mortal. Do not touch this spot.

Ponce de Leon

Who are ye, maidens?

A Daughter of the Dawn

Daughters of the Dawn.

Ponce de Leon [*gladly*]

Then by your presence I have found the place
That holds the Fountain of immortal Youth.

[36]

THE FOUNTAIN OF YOUTH

> [*As he speaks* THE GUARDIAN OF
> THE FOUNTAIN, *this time without the
> crystal cup, appears before him,
> beautiful and imperious.*]

And who art thou?

THE GUARDIAN OF THE FOUNTAIN

>   The guard perpetual,
The spirit of the Fountain callèd Youth.

PONCE DE LEON

Thine eyes hold glory that doth dazzle me!
Give me to drink.

> [*As he speaks the* DAUGHTERS OF
> THE DAWN *withdraw a little, so that
> what ensues lies between* PONCE DE
> LEON *and* THE GUARDIAN OF THE
> FOUNTAIN.]

THE GUARDIAN OF THE FOUNTAIN

>   Wilt thou snatch Youth from me?
For if this spring is touched by mortal lips
It vanisheth. No more, for all the world,
Shall there be Youth.

PLAYS OF THE PIONEERS

Ponce de Leon

And I?

The Guardian of the Fountain

              Adventurer,
Thou shalt have Youth. But think at what a cost
Thou, out of all the world, shalt Youth possess!

Ponce de Leon [*unheeding*]

Youth everlasting! Now at last I win!
I, Ponce de Leon, whom men called a fool
For following lost hopes! I win! I win!
Yea, in a moment I shall hold the cup
Within these hands and quaff supernal fire!
Guard of the Fountain—

The Guardian of the Fountain

            Wilt thou rob the world?
The sweetness and the promise of the earth?
I pray thee wait. Shall all the world lose youth
Because one man would be for ever young?
Adventurer, bethink thee what thou dost!

Ponce de Leon

Have I crossed unknown seas, and have I borne
Despair and thirst and weariness for this—

THE FOUNTAIN OF YOUTH

To hear the Guardian of the Fount itself
Cry, "Wait a little!"

[*With greatening passion.*]

              Saints! Have I not waited
And heard the tread of the invincible years
Like armies passing me? I *will* be young,
Cost what it may! Bring thou the cup to me.
I am the conqueror! I alone had faith!
And for my faith the cup is my reward!
Give me to drink, or else by this my sword
I wrest it from thee. Wilt thou serve me here,
Or must I snatch it from the fount itself?

        [*As* PONCE DE LEON *has been speak-
ing he has taken a step or two forward.
His words have drawn the* DAUGH-
TERS OF THE DAWN *forward from
sheer terror. They stand lined at
each side of* THE GUARDIAN OF THE
FOUNTAIN, *who still bars* PONCE DE
LEON'S *way. At his last words the*
DAUGHTERS OF THE DAWN *shrink
as from a blow.*]

THE DAUGHTERS OF THE DAWN [*with a cry,
               poignantly*]
Ai!

THE GUARDIAN OF THE FOUNTAIN

Inexorably my fate compels
That I must serve. I bid thee wait.

> [*Exeunt* THE GUARDIAN OF THE
> FOUNTAIN *and the* DAUGHTERS OF
> THE DAWN, *right. The first part of
> the "Idyllo" is played very faintly
> and very slowly, as if all the rapture
> had gone from it.* PONCE DE LEON,
> *left alone, speaks triumphantly.*]

PONCE DE LEON

A moment, and I am for ever young!
A Queen of Egypt melted pearls in wine.
That was a drink for slaves compared to this!

> [*Re-enter* THE GUARDIAN OF THE
> FOUNTAIN *and the* DAUGHTERS OF
> THE DAWN. *The music ceases. The*
> DAUGHTERS OF THE DAWN *stand at
> the edge of the forest.* THE GUAR-
> DIAN OF THE FOUNTAIN *approaches*
> PONCE DE LEON, *the crystal cup
> held straight before her. She speaks
> with icy scorn.*]

THE FOUNTAIN OF YOUTH

The Guardian of the Fountain

Look, thou, adventurer! Behold the cup!
Drink to the doom of youth! To glory dead!
Drink .to the ending of all loveliness!
Drink to the quenching of that sacred fire
By which the world has warmed its dying hopes
And quickered them to life again. *Drink deep!*

> [*She gives him the cup. He takes it
> exultantly, holding it upward to the
> light as one who can scarcely gaze
> his fill.* The Guardian of the
> Fountain *watches him, statue-like,
> but the* Daughters of the Dawn
> *are a frieze of alternating hope and
> despair.* Ponce de Leon *starts to
> put the cup to his lips, then hesitates.*]

Ponce de Leon [*to himself*]

Something . . . I know not what . . . would stay my
   hand.

> [*Once more he raises the cup sunward,
> then brings it toward his lips with an
> ecstatic gesture.*]

This, to my triumph!

[*He is about to drink when very faintly, like a magic whisper, the notes of the "Spring Song" steal on the air. He lowers his hand as if an echo haunted him.*]

"*Wilt thou rob the world,
The sweetness and the promise of the earth?*"

[*The music ceases.*]

Lo! How it sparkles! Mingled flame and dew! One draught! One taste!

[*He puts it resolutely to his lips.* THE GUARDIAN OF THE FOUNTAIN *and the* DAUGHTERS OF THE DAWN *veil their faces, standing like a Greek frieze. Once more the "Spring Song" echoes, a mere thread of sound.*]

"*No more for all the world
Shall there be—*"

[*He stops. The music dies.*]

Pah!

[*He turns savagely to* THE GUARDIAN OF THE FOUNTAIN.]

THE FOUNTAIN OF YOUTH

Thy words have poisoned it!
Made it a thing unclean for me to touch—
How shall I drink, knowing I rob the world?
How shall I quench the only spark of hope
The gray earth keeps?

[*Half-unbelieving joy flashes across
the faces of the* DAUGHTERS OF THE
DAWN *and* THE GUARDIAN OF THE
FOUNTAIN.]

Spirit, take back the cup!

[THE GUARDIAN OF THE FOUNTAIN
starts forward.]

No! No! I spoke in jest. Oh, bitter Youth,

[*To himself, deeply.*]

It is so short, and stays so short a time.

THE GUARDIAN OF THE FOUNTAIN [*with grave
gentleness*]
And therefore is immortal.

PONCE DE LEON [*torn*]

Ah, must I
Give up what I have searched for?

[43]

THE GUARDIAN OF THE FOUNTAIN [*immovable, but with her eyes on his*]

'Tis with thee
The matter rests.   Wilt thou condemn the world?

[*She stretches out her arms in pleading; there is a moment's silence.*]

PONCE DE LEON [*as if the words were torn from him*]

No!

THE GUARDIAN OF THE FOUNTAIN [*with passion*]

By this Fountain, spoken like a man!
This land shall ever be a land of youth
To all the nations! Thou hast purchased it,
Oh, great adventurer! Knight of Ocean-Sea,
Courageous captain!

[*She takes the cup from him.*]

PONCE DE LEON [*miserably*]

Ah, what shall I say
When men taunt: "Did ye find the goal ye sought,
Proud Ponce de Leon?   For Americus,
Cabato, and Magellan did succeed,

THE FOUNTAIN OF YOUTH

Yea, and Columbus, against heavy odds.
So, Ponce de Leon, why have ye come back
With empty hands?"   How shall I answer them
In verity?

THE GUARDIAN OF THE FOUNTAIN

Say, *I have dreamed a dream.*
Not now, but later, shall my dream come true.
So long, so long as dreamers build their dreams
Without a thought of gain shall Youth endure
Here in this land.   Oh, brave adventurer,
Face thou men's scorn as thou hast faced the waves,
And for a greater reason.   Now, farewell!

PONCE DE LEON [*his eyes on her*]

But it goes hard to part with thee at last!
Oh, Youth!   Lost Youth!   Fountain of dreams,
    farewell!

> [*He bows his head.*   THE GUARDIAN
> OF THE FOUNTAIN *with a last look
> returns to the dim forest, the* DAUGH-
> TERS OF THE DAWN *fading after her,
> a dim glimmer through the trees.
> Just as they vanish* SILVA *and*
> CORDOBA *appear at edge of woods,
> left.*   SILVA *holds a string of fish.*]

CORDOBA

We have come back. Good news! We found a
lake.

SILVA

A lake with fish in it. A mighty catch!

[*He holds up the fish.*]

CORDOBA [*rubbing his hands delightedly*]

Strength to renew the search!

PONCE DE LEON

              Nay, search no more.
It was a dream that led me, and the dream
Ends here.

> [*They are about to question him, but
> something in his demeanor stops
> them. He walks on gravely, toward
> left. They follow.*]

CORDOBA

No Fountain, Silva!

[46]

THE FOUNTAIN OF YOUTH

SILVA

And no Youth!

CORDOBA

Eh! Eh! Said I not so?

SILVA

And yet he looks
Uplift, as he had found the Fount itself!

[*To the first bars of Grieg's "Death of Ase"* THE GUARDIAN OF THE FOUNTAIN *and the attending* DAUGHTERS OF THE DAWN *look out from right in pity, then they silently withdraw.* PONCE DE LEON *and his followers exit, and the stage is left vacant.*]

MAY-DAY

MAY-DAY

CHARACTERS:

MIRIAM   DORCAS   GIDEON
DREAM FOLK (including THE MAY-DAY FOOL, THE TABORER, ROBIN
    HOOD, MAID MARIAN, and the other MORRIS-DANCERS)

PLACE—*Boston.*

TIME—*A May-day morning in the year 1658.*

SCENE—*Interior of a Puritan home. A room that
is stern in its simplicity. A hearth at right,
with a wood-fire burning. It is low and red.
Andirons. A kettle swinging on the hob.
Two three-legged iron pots a-simmer near the
fire. Also an iron bowl. A hearth broom and
bellows. A wooden settle with a high back by
the fire. It faces audience.*

    *All across the background hang dark-brown
curtains, which part in the middle to give entrance to any one coming or going. Just beyond
them is supposedly the door which gives on the*

[51]

*outer world.   At left, near foreground, a high-
back chair, facing right.   It is set very stiffly
and primly.*

At the rise of the curtain MIRIAM, *a pretty,
slender young Puritan in a gray dress, with
white cap and kerchief, is kneeling by the
hearth.   She is stirring the contents of a pot
with a long iron spoon.*

*There is the sound of a latch twitched in the
background behind curtains.* MIRIAM *raises
her head, puts down spoon, and listens.   The
sound is repeated very cautiously a second time.*

MIRIAM [*rising and listening*]

Nay, that is some one pausing at our door!
'Tis bolted safely.

[*Raises voice.*]

Who is there?   No more
A single sound.   Perhaps 'twere best to see—
Though always thoughts of Indians frighten me!

[*She runs through curtains to door,
and immediately there is the sound of
a door opening.*]

Why, Dorcas!   *Dorcas!*

MAY-DAY

[DORCAS *enters with* MIRIAM. *She is
sixteen or seventeen or thereabout, with
mischief dancing in her eyes. Her
movements are light and quick. She
carries a May-basket filled with May-
flowers and leaves. Her dress is a deep
bright blue, and her cloak likewise.*]

DORCAS

[*indicating flowers that have dropped from basket.*]

See what you have done!
Scattered my sweet bright posies, every one!

[*They pick up flowers and put basket
on hearth-shelf.*]

And I came but a May-basket to twine
Upon the latch for sake of auld lang syne.

MIRIAM

Thank you, sweet Dorcas.   Come you in and rest.

[*They go to fire.*]

DORCAS

Where are your parents, Gideon, and the rest?

[53]

PLAYS OF THE PIONEERS

Miriam

Off to town-meeting, and I bide alone,
And tend my duties. Wand'ring airs have blown
Your cap and kerchief, Dorcas, all awry.

> [DORCAS *settles these by the aid of a
> pewter plate which she takes from the
> hearth-shelf and uses as a mirror.
> She is no whit abashed by the in-
> telligence.*]

Dorcas

Then many must have seen it. There passed by
Folk from a ship new landed, old and young.
And as I looked at them my heart was wrung
With memories of England, and the gay
Sights we were wont to see there on May-day.

Miriam

Such thoughts for Puritans are scarcely meet.

Dorcas [*on settle, her eyes dancing*]

Yea, but this Puritan has wicked feet.
If they but hear a tune they wish to dance.

And I must straightway lecture them: "Advance
Not one whit further, Master Heel and Toe,
Or I, alas, into the stocks may go
For light and most unseemly wayfaring."

> [*She stretches out her feet in square-
> toed slippers, lecturing them with an
> admonishing forefinger, then tucks
> them back beneath her dress.*]

But what are we to do when it is *spring?*

Miriam

Some think e'en May-day baskets are a snare.

Dorcas [*laughing and clapping her hands*]

They are! They are! Since I have set one there
And you have sniffed at it. We're sinners, all.
But *thou* art good.

> [*She gives* Miriam *a swift caress.*]

Miriam

       Nay, nay! My spirits fall
In thinking of my sins. Oh, could you know
What I did think on but an hour ago!

DORCAS

What?

MIRIAM [*shamefacedly*]

      Oh, I longed for May-day revelry,
For morris bells and dancers and a tree
Decked like a May-pole. Oh, can I forget
May-day in England? All the hedges wet
With shining dew—the dawn flush in the skies.
Always they made me turn away mine eyes
From wickedness. But I—I used to crawl
Into a hidden spot behind the wall
And watch them—pranked in yellow and in red,
With bladders that they banged about each head,
And taborers that played a merry tune—
They always passed a-down the street too soon.

DORCAS

I know. I often stole a look at them
When dew lay on the hawthorn like a gem,
The morris-dancers came, and everywhere
They waved green ferns and branches through the
    air.
I watched the jingling fool, in motley clad:
Oh, why is it so wicked to be glad?

MIRIAM

Alas! I know not.

MAY-DAY

Dorcas

What is this you make?

Miriam

Sweet Basil brew.   "Come, let us now partake,"
As Gideon says.

[*She looks mock solemn, then smiles.*]

'Tis called Queen Mab's own drink.

Dorcas

Queen Mab!   And why is that?

Miriam

Oh, old wives think
That if you sup and wish on Basil brew
That you will surely have your wish come true.

Dorcas [*impishly*]

Come, sup!

Miriam

The elders frown on such a thing.

[57]

DORCAS

The elders are a long, long way from spring.
Come, wish.

> [MIRIAM *pours the brew into a pew-*
> *ter cup. Her guest sips first. Then*
> *they look at each other.*]

MIRIAM

What did you wish?

DORCAS

                                   I wished to see
Once more a morris-dance.

MIRIAM [*half guiltily*]

                           The same with me!
Come, sit you down beside the fire.

> [*Tosses on a fagot or two.*]

DORCAS

                             How blue
The little flames are! By a wish—come—true
It—seems—as—if—I—heard—a morris-tune.

> [*Drowsily.*]

MAY-DAY

*[The first notes of the morris-dance
are heard very faintly and delicately
played, as if coming from behind the
curtains at background.[1]]*

MIRIAM [*also drowsily*]

I—know—a—wish—could—not—come—true—so
  —soon.
Alack! I sleepy grow.

[*Nods.*]

DORCAS [*rousing herself a little*]

          And all things seem
As if they bloomed and wavered in a dream
Woven by fairy Mab with tricksy spells.

[*Faint ringing of morris-bells mingles
with the faint music.*]

I—seem—to—hear—the—sound—of—morris-
  bells.

[*They sleep, seated on the settle, their
heads together, the firelight touching
them with rosy glow. Instantly the*

---

[1] See chapter on music.

curtains are parted by THE MAY-
DAY FOOL, *clad in motley. He waves
his fool-stick, on which bells jingle
softly.*]

THE FOOL [*with a caper*]

Basil brew!
Dream come true!

[*With grandiloquent gesture he opens
the curtains on one side, and* ROBIN
HOOD *appears on the other, clad in
Lincoln green. Between the curtains come* MAID MARIAN, THE
TABORER *jingling his tabor, a tat-
tered picturesque fiddler, and all the
rest of the morris-dancers. The fiddler plays,* THE TABORER *jingles,
and all sweep into a set of morris-
dances. Morris - dance. Bobbing
Joe. Laudanum Bunches. At the
end of the dances, and with music
still playing,* THE FOOL *with a
caper crosses to where the Puritan
maids are dreaming, waves his stick
with bells over them as if breaking a
spell. Then he and* ROBIN HOOD
part the curtains, and all dance out.

[60]

MAY-DAY

The music ceases a moment after with the effect of growing fainter and farther away. MIRIAM *and* DORCAS *slowly open their eyes, stifle yawns, and are turning to look at each other when a brisk knock is heard without.*]

MIRIAM

Hark! Some one knocks!

DORCAS [*dreamy-eyed*]

    I dreamed that I had seen
A fool in motley, Robin Hood in green.

MIRIAM [*settling her cap ere she goes to the door*]

The same did I.

DORCAS [*as* MIRIAM *goes to the door*]

    And music sweet that rang
As if a thrush and fifty linnets sang!

    [*There has come the sound of a latch being lifted and a door opened.*

> Miriam *re-enters, followed by her brother* Gideon, *a long-faced young man dressed in black Puritan garb. All that he says and does is very solemn.*]

Miriam

Come in, my brother.

Gideon

Dorcas, a fair day.

Dorcas [*lightly*]

Yea, as it should be on the first of May.

Gideon

I have heard worthy talk, yea, solemn words.

Dorcas [*provocatively*]

Tell me, good Gideon, did you hear the birds? And did you know that May-flowers were in bloom?

> [Gideon *sees for the first time the May-basket on the hearth-shelf. He at once takes it and throws it into the fire.*]

[62]

MAY-DAY

GIDEON

I do not give unholy trifles room
Within my thoughts.

[*Turns to his sister.*]

And while I was away,
Miriam, tell me how you spent the day.

MIRIAM

First did I sweep.   Then filled a recipe
For Basil brew, and comfrey, and sage-tea.

GIDEON [*pompously, with a look at* DORCAS]

I wish *all* maids their time might so employ,
And find their daily tasks their only joy.
I wish all laughter banished from the earth
So folk might ponder on their little worth.
Miriam, Dorcas, what have you to say?

MIRIAM [*very demurely*]

I beg you not to wish on a May-day.

[*She looks down piously.*]

DORCAS [*looking full at him, and speaking with subtle sweetness*]

*Or if you wish, in wishing see that you
Do not drink deeply of sweet Basil brew!*

[63]

THE VANISHING RACE

This play formed the second episode of the Historical Pageant of Schenectady, New York, which that city united with Union College in giving as a three-day celebration of the two-hundred-and-fiftieth anniversary of the founding of the town. The pageant was staged on the college grounds with a background of woods suggesting the forest primeval. Through this wood, running down to the edge of the pageant grounds, was an old Indian trail used by the Five Nations from time immemorial. Near this vicinity was the reputed site of the old Mohawk castle, and on this very spot Arent van Curler, as in the play, made his purchase of land from the Indians. In the play many of the words spoken by the characters are taken verbatim from old letters, diaries, and histories of the time. The scene is typical of Dutch pioneers — of their steady progress and sagacity, of their complacent stolidity which saw nothing of the tragedy of the vanishing race that was enacted before their eyes. Arent van Curler was one of the most important figures in the history of New York State. See *The Jesuits in North America*, by Francis Parkman, and *History of the United States*, by E. Benjamin Andrews, for adequate descriptions of the time.

THE VANISHING RACE[1]

CHARACTERS:

SAWARA (an Indian medicine-woman)
KASWI (an Indian)
KENNISGKE (an Indian chieftain)
OCHEE (a lesser chieftain)
ARENT VAN CURLER
NICK VAN VALSEN
JAN WEMP   } Dutch pioneers
PETER VAN SLYCK

Indian chieftains and braves. Indian maidens, women, and children.

TIME—*1662*.

PLACE—*The home of the Five Nations, New York State.*

SCENE—*A cleared space in a forest.*

> *The cleared space in the forest has trees right, left, and background. An Indian trail leads directly up background to the "Castle" or home of the Five Nations that stood on the site of what is now the modern city of Schenectady. The*

[1] Copyright, 1912, by Constance D'Arcy MacKay.

[67]

castle is not seen, as it is farther back in the forest.

There are two wigwams at right, one in background, and three at left. Rude bowls for holding corn. Two slender poles with a willow-bark rope between them on which some pieces of venison are drying. A fire at right. The wigwam that is farthest to the right has red cabalistic signs on its door. Some corn and a squash lie just at the door, as if left there as a gift.

The play begins with the entrance of a group of laughing Indian maidens who seat themselves in a semicircle, background. An old Indian enters, and one of the maidens runs up to him and apparently begs him for something. He disappears into a wigwam at the left, and appears again with an old and battered Indian war-drum. Sitting by the door of the wigwam, he beats out a barbaric measure on it, and an Indian maiden who has just come in with an armful of the first yellow leaves of autumn imitates the whirling of the falling leaves in a brief dance pantomime, which the other Indian maidens watch, half teasing her.[1] The dance ends, and the maiden is crossing toward the old Indian when SAWARA appears in the background, a magnificently picturesque Indian

[1] See chapter on music.

*woman of middle years, tall and straight, wear-
ing, besides her Indian dress, gorgeous neck-
laces and armlets, and a black and white blanket
curiously woven. The Indian maidens give
way before her with gestures of obeisance.
SAWARA inclines her head gravely and goes
directly to wigwam at right where the decorated
door is. The Indian maidens retire to extreme
left, where they sit laughing and chattering in
pantomime. KASWI enters from right, a shifty-
eyed Indian. He approaches SAWARA with too
great humility. He speaks to her haltingly, as
one who would make himself familiar with the
tongue of the Palefaces.*

KASWI. Speak in the tongue of—the Palefaces,
Sawara, that—I—may—also—learn—to—speak—
it. [SAWARA *looks straight before her.*] You—who
—have—lived—near—the houses—of the Palefaces, and—have—the—gift—of—tongues—you
—who—are—the—medicine-woman, and—very—
wise. [*Pleadingly.*] As—a—favor, Sawara. [*He
puts a bunch of herbs beside the other gifts that lie by
her wigwam.*] As—a—favor, Sawara! [*She will
not look at him.*] In—the—winter—Kaswi—
brought—many beaver-skins—to—the—door—of
the wigwam of Sawara. A gift for a gift, Sawara.
[*He pauses, looking at her craftily.*]

SAWARA [*with great dignity*]. A gift for a gift, Kaswi. You are over-anxious to speak in the tongue of the Palefaces. It bodes ill for one nation to copy another nation. As for the tongue of the Paleface, it will soon be the only tongue we shall hear. [*Bitterly.*] Our own tongue will be no more remembered than the song of the cricket when summer is over.

KASWI. You who have lived near the houses of the Palefaces—

SAWARA [*proudly*]. If I have lived near the houses of the Palefaces it was not of my own choosing. [*She wheels on him, head thrust forth like a snake about to strike, her eyes glittering and narrowing as she hisses the words at him.*] I can tell you why you are anxious to learn their tongue, Kaswi. It is so you can do better trading. [*They face each other for an instant. Then* SAWARA *turns from him, and on impulse turns back again.*] A gift for a gift, Kaswi. My gift is given.

> [*She enters her wigwam, only appearing again when the Dutch pioneers arrive. While she has been speaking Indian braves and chiefs come in from left with a few trophies of the hunt, a rabbit or two and some birds. The Indian women, followed by*

*children, come in from background
with wild apples and herbs. The
whole camp is full of movement and
color. The Indian women are has-
tening to replenish the fire with wood;
others are grinding corn between
stones. One of them is weaving a
basket; another is weaving a blanket;
still another is hanging a papoose up
in a tree, while the Indian maidens
stand laughingly beneath it.*

*[From the woods in left appear the
Dutch pioneers on horseback. They
are* ARENT VAN CURLER, VAN VAL-
SEN, *a miller,* JAN WEMP, *and* PETER
VAN SLYCK. *The braves see them,
and point them out with exclamations:
"Ugh! Ugh!" The Indian women
and maidens cease their duties and
chatter.* SAWARA, *aware of something unusual, looks out and comes
forward.* JAN WEMP *leads a pack-
horse to whose sides are strapped
kegs of gunpowder. The men tether
their horses at right and come forward
to center,* VAN CURLER *in the lead.
The Indian women go to background.
The Indian men remain stolidly in*

their places. SAWARA seats herself alone at the far left, forward. She watches all that takes place.]

VAN CURLER. Greetings to the chiefs of the Mohawks.

KENNISGKE. The chiefs give greeting to their "very good friend," Van Curler.

OCHEE. Van Curler smoke peace-pipe with Mohawks.

[*The Indians assemble for council. A great circle is formed about the fire. The peace-pipe is lit and passed. SAWARA rises and crosses to the door of her own wigwam, where she sits waiting. As those in council speak they rise from the circle, then seat themselves again.*]

VAN CURLER. Greetings to you, O chiefs, from Van Curler and from the Big Chief, Governor Peter Stuyvesant, with whose knowledge I have come to you. Not alone have I come to your council. With me are my friends Jan Wemp, Van Slyck, and the miller Van Valsen. They, too, would speak with you, knowing you friends of the Palefaces.

KENNISGKE. The friends of Van Curler are welcome.

THE VANISHING RACE

OCHEE. There are none more wise than Van Curler.

VAN CURLER [*flatteringly*]. There are none greater than the Sachems who are chiefs of the Tribe of the Bear. Their hatchets are as keen as the north wind and their eyes are as eagles' eyes. [*Offers wampum.*] Will Kennisgke accept a gift from his friend Van Curler? [*Offers great strings of beads.* KENNISGKE *grunts, and offers a beaver-skin in return.*]

VAN CURLER. We thank the chief for his gift.

KENNISGKE. Will the corlear [1] rest after his long journey? Let food be brought to him and to his friends.

[*Indian maidens run down with food and drink, venison and water.*]

VAN CURLER. The women of the tribe of the Mohawks are fair and gentle, and the warriors strong.

KENNISGKE. Let our white brother speak his mind.

VAN CURLER. Friends, it is long since I came to this new country to direct that portion of it belonging to Killean van Rensselaer the patroon, my uncle. It is twenty years since I first saw

[1] A term of respect.

Shonowe.[1] It was fair then. It is not less fair now.

KENNISGKE. We listen.

VAN CURLER. But we men of Beverwick and Rensselaer grow weary of the place we dwell in. We speak to our brothers, the Sachems, freely, knowing them to be of our mind, knowing that they love justice and freedom.

OCHEE. The corlear speaks truly.

VAN CURLER. We would found a settlement where all men would be free and equal, where the men would say "we" and "our" instead of "my" and "mine."

SEVERAL OF THE YOUNG BRAVES. Good counsel! The Sachems listen.

VAN VALSEN. Furthermore, we are not altogether free. There are those who rule our coming and going, the great East India Company, of which my brothers have already heard. We would lessen the weight of that yoke also. We speak to our brothers in confidence, knowing they know us of old.

KENNISGKE [*gravely*]. What the chieftains have heard with their ears will not go out by way of their tongues.

VAN CURLER [*gaining confidence*]. Therefore, my

[1] Early name of Schenectady, given by the Indians and meaning "Land beyond the Pine Plains."

brothers, we have come to you for two reasons. One, because we know you and trust you, and because your land is fair; the other, *because we know that game is scarce in your borders*. The guns of the Paleface have killed it. The time will come when you will not dwell in Shonowe. If my brothers *must* sell, why not sell to their very good friend? [*Silence. The Indians smoke imperturbably*.] What say the chiefs of the Mohawks?

KENNISGKE. I make answer to the corlear: Does a man sell his home? Does he quench his hearth-fire for strangers?

[SAWARA *leans forward, listening passionately*.]

ALL BRAVES. Wah! No! No!
VAN CURLER. You will not sell?
ALL BRAVES [*loudly*]. No!

[SAWARA's *face shows deep joy*.]

KENNISGKE. Brothers, shall we not keep our castle, the home of the great Five Nations?
ALL BRAVES [*with one accord*]. Yes!
VAN CURLER. Have I ever deceived you, my brothers, or spoken untruly?
ALL BRAVES. Never, corlear.

VAN CURLER. Or cheated you, or made a bad bargain?

OCHEE. No. The corlear is always honest.

VAN CURLER [*impressively*]. Then listen to me now, for I am telling you the truth. If you do not deal with me the time is coming when you must deal with others. There is wisdom in what I say, Sachems. We will give you a just price for your land, and we will build our farms on it. Do not be hasty in refusing, for it will be as I have said. Will my brothers talk with the tribe? There are new lands for them to the westward.

[*The council breaks up. VAN CUR-*
LER and his followers confer at left.
The Indians confer at right.]

VAN CURLER. If the chiefs consent to sell their land there will be room for fifteen farms and for each man a pasture to the east of the village and a garden to the south of the village, and we will call the place Schenectady, and in our tongue it will mean "Beautiful Valley."[1]

VAN VALSEN [*looking at the Indians*]. What are they doing?

VAN SLYCK. They are calling out a medicine-woman to go before their gods for them. It is a

[1] Actual words.

custom they have. They will decide by the magic sticks.

> [*It is seen that* KENNISGKE *summons* SAWARA *by gesture, bidding her to the council fire. She shakes her head. Again, by gesture, he commands her. She begins to cross slowly toward the fire.*]

VAN VALSEN. I have heard of her before time. They say she has the gift of tongues, and once lived near the white folk of our village. The Indians hold her in great honor. They say she can foretell the future.

WEMP [*piously*]. It is necromancy! I will have none of it.

> [*The Dutch pioneers retire to left.* SAWARA *and the Indians gather at right to the notes of MacDowell's "From an Indian Lodge." The music rises, then dies.*]

KENNISGKE. Speak, Sawara. You who have dwelt near the houses of the Palefaces, you who have the gift of tongues. What will become of it, Sawara? Prophesy. Speak in the tongue of the Palefaces.

SAWARA [*facing audience as one who sees dimly the first of a vision*]. The land shall be sold, but for us no good will come of it. But the man who wishes to buy it is a good man. He will prosper.

KENNISGKE. But for us, Sawara—

SAWARA. You have seen the graying ashes of the camp-fire. When the white man comes only the ashes will be left to us. [*She falls silent.*]

OCHEE. Speak in the tongue of the Paleface.

SAWARA. What shall I speak when my heart is as twisted as a willow-tree in the wind? Shall I make a medicine when my spirit is gone from me? [*Yet she takes the first few steps of the medicine dance at the fire to the rhythm of MacDowell's music. KASWI approaches and throws on a bundle of the magic sticks. Blue and green flames are seen to rise and flicker. SAWARA's voice becomes that of a prophetess. Her eyes see visions.*]

I sing the song of my people,
I sing the grief of my people.
You will sell the land to the Paleface,
For what will be will be.
There is no help for it.
Our hunting-grounds are deserted,
There are few fish left in the streams—
We must go or starve.
We must sell the land to the Paleface.

THE VANISHING RACE

A hundred hundred years has our tribe trodden the
    trail.
They shall tread it no more.
A hundred hundred years has the smoke gone up
    from these wigwams—
The years are over.
You will sell the land to the Paleface—
He will dwell where once was your dwelling.
For a few years you will flourish,
And then there will be no more strength in you
    than there is in a wet bow-string.
Our faces are turned toward the sunset.
The shadows gather around us.
What will be will be.
There is no help for it.
I sing the song of my people.
I sing the grief of my people.

> [SAWARA *ceases and moves back from
> the camp-fire. The Mohawks ·are
> depressed.*]

KENNISGKE. This is woman talk, Sawara.

SAWARA. It may be a woman speaks truly.

OCHEE. She has the gift of tongues and can
prophesy. What will be will be.

SAWARA. Never came good of greed. [*She
stands apart from her people.*]

KENNISGKE. Corlear, it is hard to answer. If we sell to you you will deal with us fairly. It is true that game is scarce, and our hunters are long in finding it. It is true that there are new lands to the westward. [*To Indians.*] My brothers, if what must be must be, let us sell to our very good friends. [SAWARA *hides her face with her blanket.*] What say you?

THE BRAVES. Let us sell.

VAN CURLER. Great Chief, I will deal with you fairly. For your lands we will give you four kegs of the gunpowder that the Mohawks so greatly prize.

KENNISGKE. It is enough. We will make our brothers welcome. We will move our wigwams westward. We will quench our camp-fire.

VAN CURLER. Then let us sign the charter.

> [*A roll of parchment, quill pen, and ink-horn are brought by* VAN VALSEN. *The Dutch pioneers and the two Indians sign the charter. The horse with the kegs of gunpowder is approached by the Indians and the kegs unstrapped. While the men are signing the charter the wigwams are taken down, the squaws and maidens gathering their blankets and cooking-*

utensils. Young braves take down and carry the wigwams—there is no time now for the women to do all the work. The men march first, single file, the squaws, maidens, and children following in groups of ones and twos. Again the notes of "From an Indian Lodge" are played. It is evident that the never-ending march westward has begun. The last Indian to leave is SAWARA, *looking straight before her.*]

VAN CURLER. Come. Let us choose a spot on which to build our farms.

[*The pioneers mount their horses and ride away.*]

6

THE PASSING OF HIAWATHA

This play formed the opening episode of the Historical Pageant of Schenectady, New York, which that city united with Union College in giving as a three-day celebration of the two-hundred-and-fiftieth anniversary of the founding of the town. The pageant was staged on the college grounds with a background of woods suggesting the forest primeval. Through this wood, running down to the edge of the pageant grounds, was an old Indian trail, used by the Five Nations from time immemorial. Near this vicinity was the reputed site of the famous Mohawk "castle." But why Hiawatha in this vicinity? the reader will ask. The following paragraph will explain. It is taken from an article by Mr. Horatio Hale in the Proceedings of the American Academy for the Advancement of Science.

"Hiawatha was a chief of the Onondagas,[1] who succeeded in bringing about a league or union of the Five, afterward Six, Nations. . . . Mr. Schoolcraft transferred the hero to a distant region, identifying him with a divinity of the Ojibways.

[1] Modern Schenectady stands on their former hunting-ground.

It is to this (Mr. Schoolcraft's) collection that we owe the poem of Longfellow."

But so great is the power of poetry in coloring fact that popular knowledge will always associate Hiawatha with the "land of the Big Sea Water"— the Great Lakes. Therefore in preparing this play for general producing the author has substituted Ojibway instead of Mohawk names throughout, and has placed the play in the land of Longfellow's poem so as to avoid confusion, realizing that the average community in giving the play will wish to adhere to the traditions that they already know, unvexed and unpuzzled by any thought of origins.

THE PASSING OF HIAWATHA[1]

CHARACTERS:

HIAWATHA

PEZHE-KEE

SA-JA-WUN

ME-DA-KEE-WIS

AHMEEK

OWEENEE

WABENOWUSK ⎱ Little boys
ADJIDAMUS ⎰

BRIGHT FLOWER

STAR OF SPRINGTIME

MISKODEED

THE CHIEF OF THE OMAHAS

THE CHIEF OF THE DACOTAHS

THE CHIEF OF THE BLACKFEET

THE CHIEF OF THE PAWNEES

THE CHIEF OF THE CHOCTAWS

HERON'S PLUME (a young brave)

THE SPIRITS OF THE SUNSET

Other braves and warriors. Indian maidens and women. Indian children.

TIME—*1670.*

PLACE—*St. Esprit, near La Pointe, on the western extremity of Lake Superior.*

SCENE—*An Indian encampment. Wigwams in the background and a camp-fire at right.*

The play opens with the entrance of AHMEEK, *an old medicine-man, and* ME-DA-KEE-WIS, *an old flute-player, deep in talk. Two squaws*

[1] Copyright, 1912, by Constance D'Arcy MacKay.

enter; one begins to grind corn, another hangs a papoose up in a tree. A group of Indian maidens enter from background; some of them have baskets for weaving, but they pay more attention to chattering together than to work. Presently comes OWEENEE, *a woman of middle years and great importance in the camp. On her back is a bundle of fagots. She looks keenly at the idle maidens.*

OWEENEE

Star of Springtime, take the fagots.

> [STAR OF SPRINGTIME *does as she is bid; tosses fagots on fire.*]

In my youth I was not idle,
Did not spend my time in gazing
Upward at the birch-tree branches.

> [*Maidens under this reproach work with furious industry.* OWEENEE *takes a loom and begins to weave at center.*]

STAR OF SPRINGTIME [*pouting*]

Oweenee is ever scolding!
Like an arrowhead her tongue is!

THE PASSING OF HIAWATHA

[*A group of Indian children rush in from background, almost overturning* OWEENEE'S *weaving-frame in their play.*]

OWEENEE [*severely*]

Children who disturb their elders
Will be turned to little rabbits.
Think of this, O Wabenowusk,
And you, too, O Adjidamus!

[*Little Indian boys retire abashed.*]

AN INDIAN MAIDEN

Where is Bright Flower?

SECOND INDIAN MAIDEN

She is coming.

[BRIGHT FLOWER *appears in background.*]

In the brook she saw her likeness,
Paused to watch it and admire it.

[STAR OF SPRINGTIME *laughs.*]

PLAYS OF THE PIONEERS

Bright Flower

If I told tales on my neighbors
I might say much, Star of Springtime.

Miskodeed

Here comes Pezhe-kee, the hunter.
He has spent the Moon of Leafage
In the land beyond the river.

> [Pezhe-kee *enters from left, and,
> seating himself near* Oweenee, *tosses
> a pack of skins from his back.*]

Oweenee

It is long since we have seen you.
Greetings, friend.

Pezhe-kee

      And to you, also.
All the Month of Leaves I hunted
In the land beyond the river.
Fur and feathers I was seeking,
Feathers for the arrow-maker,
Skins to keep us warm in winter.

THE PASSING OF HIAWATHA

And for one who maketh medicine
Bear's claws for a magic necklace.

> [*He crosses to right and presents
> necklace to* AHMEEK, *then returns to*
> OWEENEE, *stretching his lithe young
> length on the grass.*]

It is good to see our wigwams,
Good to see the smoke ascending.
Very pleasant is our northland,
Very sweet the murmuring forest.
But I find the camp deserted.

OWEENEE

The young braves have gone to forage.

PEZHE-KEE

Tell me, where is Hiawatha?

OWEENEE

He is gone into the forest
There to fast and to petition
The Great Spirit for his people.
Later, when the hour is ready,

He will summon to these wigwams
The great chieftains of the nations;
He will call a camp-fire council,
And the chiefs will smoke the peace-pipe.
On a hilltop far and lonely
Hiawatha keeps his vigil.
While below him, in the shadow,
Waits Sa-ja-wun, the swift runner.
At a sign from Hiawatha
Will Sa-ja-wun come to tell us
That the council fire be lighted,
That the great chiefs are approaching.

PEZHE-KEE

Wisely Hiawatha rules us,
He the son of fair Wenonah.
He descended from the West Wind.

OWEENEE

All the green month of New Leafage
Has he been apart and silent;
And toward evening by his wigwam
He has sat with face uplifted
Looking toward the Land of Sunset;
Sat as one who hears strange voices
Calling, calling through the twilight.

THE PASSING OF HIAWATHA

And my heart grows very heavy.
No, I will not think upon it.

[*Resumes work.*]

There may be no cause for sorrow.
I will give my thoughts to labor.

[*Turns sharply.*]

In the mean time Indian maidens
Need not let their hands be idle!

[*Indian maidens cease chattering and
fall to work.* OWEENEE *rises, puts
away her work, and, taking a basket
for herbs, exits background. Instantly the maidens show their joy.
Work is abandoned.*]

MISKODEED

She is gone! Oh, in my pulses
I can feel the pulse of springtime!
Let us dance, O lovely Bright Flower,
To the flute of Me-da-kee-wis!

BRIGHT FLOWER

Plead with him, O Star of Springtime!
Tell him that we love his music
Better than we love the south wind!

PLAYS OF THE PIONEERS

STAR OF SPRINGTIME

Play to us, O Me-da-kee-wis,
You alone who know the flute notes
That can move our feet to dancing.
Play to us, O Me-da-kee-wis!

> [ME-DA-KEE-WIS [*plays*, AHMEEK
> *with his medicine-drum beating time.*]

MISKODEED

Bright Flower, let us dance the Corn Dance,
Let us dance the Dance of Planting
Softly as the wind through corn-fields,
Tossing as the silken tassels,
Swaying as the rustling corn-stalks.

BRIGHT FLOWER [*joyfully*]

Dance as at the feast of planting,
Or the great feast of Mondamin!
Miskodeed, bring forth the corn-stalks!

> [MISKODEED *hastens to bring forth
> some corn on the stalk. Their first
> dance sways like a dance of harvest,
> with few steps, but with bending of*

> *the body. When this ends they put by the corn and begin the second or corn-planting dance. They stoop to the music in long rows, each maiden pretending to take kernels of corn from a basket which she carries, planting it in the earth, treading the earth over it to music. Then they lift the next kernels skyward, as if imploring the blessing of the Great Spirit, then plant them and tread them, passing forward with these gestures till the end of the music.]*

STAR OF SPRINGTIME

Play again, O Me-da-kee-wis!

> *[A sound of the war-drum is heard faintly from left.]*

BRIGHT FLOWER

Listen! Is it Hiawatha?

MISKODEED

> *[Running to look from background.]*

No! It is the Braves returning!
They are feathered for the war-path!

All their tomahawks are ready!
Let us stay and see the war-dance.

> [*Indian maidens sit in background.*
> *Braves enter from right.*]

> [*They go straight to* ME-DA-KEE-WIS,
> *led by* HERON'S PLUME.]

HERON'S PLUME

Play to us, O Me-da-kee-wis!
Ahmeek, dance for us the war-dance.

AHMEEK [*tranquilly*]

Why this war-talk? We are peaceful.

HERON'S PLUME

On the borders of our nation
We have seen a tribe of strangers.
They are like to the Comanches
And—

AHMEEK

How big a tribe? Speak truly.
Speak! ·

THE PASSING OF HIAWATHA

HERON'S PLUME [*sullenly*]

Ahmeek, they are a small tribe.
But a small tribe may breed mischief.

AHMEEK

What are we, the great Ojibways,
That the coming or the going
Of a small tribe should make interest?

HERON'S PLUME [*still sullen*]

We would be upon the war-path!

ME-DA-KEE-WIS

Ahmeek, hark! The spring is on them;
In our youth the blood runs quickly.
Let them have their war-dance, Ahmeek.

> [AHMEEK *gives a grunt of assent,
> swings his medicine-stick, and moves
> to fire, where he takes the first steps
> of a medicine-dance,* ME-DA-KEE-
> WIS *tapping on the drum.*]

THE BRAVES [*delighted*]

Medicine! Ai yi! He makes it!

7

[The drum-tapping grows louder and more barbaric. The braves swing into circle and presently are leaping in the war-dance. They rush off background, but before the camp has settled down again SA-JA-WUN *enters.]*

AHMEEK

Comes Sa-ja-wun, the swift runner.

SA-JA-WUN [*panting*]

Ahmeek, where are all the warriors?
Hiawatha bids me tell you
That he calls the braves to council,
The great chieftains of the nations.
Hiawatha's fast is ended.
He will speak to us in council.

AHMEEK

The young braves are on the war-path.
Turn them homeward, fleet Sa-ja-wun.

SA-JA-WUN

I will speed me like an arrow!

[98]

THE PASSING OF HIAWATHA

[He darts away, background. From left in full panoply come the chieftains of the nations, one by one.]

ME-DA-KEE-WIS

Come the great chiefs of the nations,
Come the Pawnees and the Blackfeet,
The Dacotahs and Shoshones,
Omahas, and for Ojibways
Last of all comes—Hiawatha.

[As the chieftains pass the council fire a great murmur of admiration goes up from the camp: "Hiawatha! Hiawatha!"]

HIAWATHA

Greetings to you, O my people.
Greetings, O you mighty chieftains.
Let us smoke the pipe together.
Let the council fire be lighted.
Where are all the younger warriors?

AHMEEK

Fleet Sa-ja-wun runs to bring them.

[*As* HIAWATHA *goes on speaking*
SA-JA-WUN *and the young warriors
return and seat themselves in council.*]

HIAWATHA

Brothers, I have much to tell you.
When I heard the Spirit call me
Many days I prayed and fasted
On a hilltop, far and lonely,
Till great Manitou, the mighty,
Sent this message: "Hiawatha,
Leave the trail and leave the hunting,
Leave the camp-fire and the wigwam,
Turn unto the Land of Sunset,
Bid farewell to all the nations,
For your time with them is ended."

INDIAN WOMEN [*a soft wail in background*]

Hiawatha! Hiawatha!

HIAWATHA

Thus said Manitou, the mighty:
"From the East, the Land of Morning,
Come the Palefaces, the Black Robes,
With strange knowledge in their keeping.

THE PASSING OF HIAWATHA

Other gods they bid you worship,
Strange new ways they bid you follow.
From the meadows and the rivers
Float the echoes of their building—
All the building of strange wigwams
Such as you have never fashioned.
As their hearth-fire groweth stronger
Yours diminisheth and weakens;
As their hearth-fire leaps and dances
Yours must fade to graying ashes.
From the east, the Land of Sunrise,
They have come, the strange Palefaces.
To the west, the Land of Sunset,
Turn your eyes, O Hiawatha!"

INDIAN WOMEN [*wailing softly*]

Wahanowin! Hiawatha!

HIAWATHA

But before I go, my brothers,
I have words to say in parting.

> [*The chieftains who are sitting in
> council rise as they are addressed.
> Then sit again.*]

You, the Pawnees and the Blackfeet,
Keep contentment in your wigwams.
See your tribes-folk do not wrangle,
Live in peace with one another,
Peace and plenty. I have spoken.

Shoshones' great chieftain, harken!
Govern all your people wisely.
Be a light unto the nations.
Light is wisdom. I have said it.

You, the chief of the Dacotahs,
See your people live in honor.
Let their word be feared and trusted
By the nations. I have said it.

Omahas' great chieftain, listen!
Teach your people that the war-drum
Is not better than the peace-pipe
Unless war is truly needed.
Grow and prosper. I have said it.

You, the people called Ojibway,
Keep alive your nation's valor,
Keep alive the old traditions
As a fire before your wigwams.
Truth and justice—seek these always.
These remember. I have spoken.

THE PASSING OF HIAWATHA

[As HIAWATHA *has been speaking the last lines to the overture of "Hiawatha's Departure," by Coleridge Taylor, there appear at right mystic figures clothed in the pale and deeper rose of sunset. They weave a mysterious dance with gestures that call and beckon.]*

STAR OF SPRINGTIME *[fearfully]*

Who are these that steal upon us?
Who are these that wave and beckon?

OWEENEE

'Tis the Spirits of the Sunset
Come to summon Hiawatha.

THE FIRST SPIRIT *[calling mystically]*

Hiawatha!

[Her voice echoes faintly like a bell-chime.]

HIAWATHA

I am ready.

THE TRIBE

Do not leave us, Hiawatha.

PLAYS OF THE PIONEERS

HIAWATHA

Fare you well, O much-loved people,
As I pass you will pass also
When the Sunset Spirits call you.

THE TRIBE

Fare you well, O Hiawatha.
Never shall your tribe forget you.

THE WOMEN [*wailing softly*]

Hiawatha! Hiawatha!

> [HIAWATHA *follows* THE SPIRITS OF
> THE SUNSET, *and they disappear,
> moving before him in the distance,
> he following.*]

THE CHIEF OF THE DACOTAHS [*gravely*]

Come and pray to the Great Spirit.

> [*Exeunt* OMNES, *background, the men
> first, the women next, then the maid-
> ens, and last of all the children.*]

DAME GREEL O' PORTLAND TOWN

This play was the seventh episode in the Historical Pageant of Portland, Maine, given on the Eastern Promenade of that city as a municipal civic celebration July 4, 1913. Since first writing the play has undergone several changes. In the first place, in Portland it was given out of doors, with greensward underfoot and pine-trees and the Atlantic Ocean for a background. It represented the inn yard of Dame Greel's tavern, and not the interior—an inn yard supplied with chairs and tables where visitors could talk and bask in the sun, served by Dame Alice and her servant-boys. In rehearsal it was found that the acoustics of the vast amphitheater in which the pageant was given, and which easily seated twenty-five thousand people, made it advisable to cut all dialogue to a minimum. Therefore, the minuet and the chatter of the colonial maids was transferred to a scene welcoming Gov. John Hancock and Dorothy Quincy Hancock, which occurred later in the pageant, and in their place was substituted a meeting of citizens—men, women, and children —assembled in Dame Greel's yard—a scene impossible to convey on the average amateur stage, where casts seldom run to more than seventy-five or a hundred persons, but easy enough to manage on a stage such as that of Portland, with a thousand pageant players to draw from. Dame Greel was one of the most famous women tavern-keepers of her day, a true patriot whom history represents as culling cannon-balls while the bombardment of Portland was going on, picking them up on a huge shovel and setting them to cool, that they might later be remelted into bullets for the American army.

DAME GREEL O' PORTLAND TOWN [1]

CHARACTERS:

DAME ALICE GREEL

POLLY PRUE JANICE ABIGAIL } Maids of Portland Town	MR. PRESTON MR. CARLYLE MR. WYNNE MR. NORTON } Tories	

MR. PREBLE (Chairman of the Committee of Safety)

MR. FOX
MR. MAYO } Members of the Committee of Safety
MR. BRADBURY

AMERICAN MESSENGER   BRITISH MESSENGER

NAT
JACK
WILL } Inn boys who serve Dame Alice Greel
TOM

TIME—*Summer, 1775.*

PLACE—DAME ALICE GREEL'S *tavern at Portland, Maine. A room wainscoted in dark woodwork. Smoke-stained walls and rafters. A large door in background, with windows each side of it. A door down stage, right. Another door up*

[1] Copyright, 1913, by Constance D'Arcy MacKay.

stage, right. These lead to other parts of the house. A wide-mouthed chimney at right, with a spark of fire. On the chimney-shelf pewter candlesticks and pewter plates. A musket hung above these, with a powder-horn. A serving-table against the left wall, with a pewter flagon and a dozen pewter cups on a tray. Other pieces of pewter and silverware.

At the rise of the curtain Tom *is sweeping the hearth and yawning. Enter from door at upper right* Dame Greel, *a brisk, bright-eyed capable woman of five-and-thirty. She at once cuffs* Tom, *takes the broom from him, and wields it herself.*

Dame Greel. Be brisk, you young laggard! There's the silver and pewter to polish. Get to thy labor and stop yawning! [*He goes, gets silver and rag, and sits down to polish.*] Here you are with breakfast over and the sleep scarce out o' your eyes. [Polly *opens the door, background, enters and courtesies.* Dame Greel *courtesies also.*] Give you good morrow, Polly Upton. What brings you out so early?

Polly. Can any lie in bed when the thought of trouble is abroad in the land? A harbor town is a dangerous place for good Americans these days. We can rise to the peril on land, but 'tis hard to withstand the peril by sea. No one knows what that treacherous Captain Mowatt, who once threatened us, may do. Rumor says he may appear any day in these waters.

> [*She has left the door wide open behind her, and there enter through it* PRUE, JANICE, *and* ABIGAIL, *all maidens of sixteen or seventeen. They courtesy to* DAME GREEL, *who bows to them in turn.*]

ABIGAIL. Good morrow, Dame Greel.

DAME GREEL [*to* ABIGAIL]. Good morrow. [*To the others.*] Good morrow.

JANICE. One would think the world was all serene to see *your* face.

DAME GREEL. The face is a bad place to wear your troubles. I keep mine in my heart.

PRUE. I try to. But they're always escaping.

DAME GREEL. What is it now?

PRUE. Oh, it discourages me to think how little women can do when anything momentous happens.

DAME GREEL. D'ye call what we do *little*?

PRUE [*in a sweet, childish voice*]. We have no strength at all.

DAME GREEL. We've the strength of good

sound wits if we want to use 'em. And that's as good as the strength o' muscle any day.

PRUE. Oh, I mean things like—like helping our Committee of Safety. They've been trying for three days to convey a store of ammunition to Mr. Fox's cellar, and they haven't succeeded yet.

DAME GREEL [*with spirit*]. What's to prevent 'em?

PRUE [*wide-eyed and with impressiveness*]. Dame Alice, don't you *know* that Mr. Preston lives right next door to Mr. Fox—Sam Preston, the greatest Tory in Portland?

JANICE. I never saw the beat of these Tories for getting in the way. They're always passing when you least expect 'em.

DAME GREEL [*as she dusts hearth-shelf and its belongings*]. Or wasting their days in idleness. Faith, they're in and out all day long, Preston and Norton, Carlyle and Wynne. Tories, every one of 'em.

JANICE. *Here?*

DAME GREEL. Yes, here.

POLLY. Oh, Janice, if we could only keep them here awhile the ammunition might be moved, and Dame Greel could send word to Mr. Fox, and—

PRUE, JANICE, ABIGAIL. But how? But how?

POLLY [*her head on one side, regarding her likeness*

in a pewter plate]. Well, we're not so ill to look at, when it comes to that!

DAME GREEL [*briskly*]. Umph! Those Tories will need more anchor than a pretty face, I'll warrant you.

POLLY [*excitedly*]. Oh, tell us, Dame Greel. Tell us! What other anchor? [*Dropping her voice.*] D'ye mean—liquor?

DAME GREEL [*practically*]. Lud! No! Liquor sets folk *drifting*. [*With a nod of certainty.*] I mean a heel-and-toe anchor.

PRUE. Dancing! Surely you don't mean *dancing*?

DAME GREEL. I surely do. And Tom can pick at a fiddle monstrous fine; can't 'ee, Tom?

> [TOM *nods. Drops his cleaning.
> From lower shelf of table takes out a
> fiddle just as from door in background
> enter* MR. CARLYLE, MR. PRESTON,
> MR. NORTON, *and* MR. WYNNE,
> *young Tories very foppish in their
> appearance, with a great showing of
> buckles and ruffles. They have gay,
> light, easy manners. Their bows at
> seeing the young ladies are of the
> most courtly. The girls, for their
> part, courtesy to the floor.* DAME
> GREEL *only half etches one.*]

MR. PRESTON [*gaily*]. What's this I hear of fiddling?

MR. NORTON [*to* DAME GREEL, *indicating the young ladies*]. Why didn't you tell us you kept a flower-garden?

MR. WYNNE [*looking at them with dandified air*]. Roses are ever my favorites.

POLLY. Best beware of thorns!

MR. PRESTON. But what's this I hear of fiddling?

POLLY. We're trying to persuade Tom to play for us. We're all mad to learn the newest steps from London.

MR. CARLYLE [*eagerly*]. And we're all mad to teach them, I do assure you!

PRUE [*primly*]. 'Tis most fortunate!

> [*Tables and chairs are moved back.* TOM *begins to play a minuet.*[1] *The sound of the music attracts* JACK, *who enters from right.* DAME GREEL *motions to him. The dancers are too engrossed to perceive her.*]

DAME GREEL [*giving paper to* JACK]. Take this to Mr. Fox, and briskly. Let none stop you on the way.

[1] Beethoven's "Minuet in G."

[*Exit* JACK *by door upper right.*
DAME GREEL *sits by hearth, knitting
tranquilly. The dance continues to
the end, then stops with a grand
flourish.*]

ABIGAIL. La! I do believe I've got it! You're
a fine teacher, Mr. Carlyle.

MR. CARLYLE [*pleased at her words*]. With an
apt pupil!

[*The young ladies move toward the
door*].

MR. PRESTON [*to* POLLY]. You're not leaving us
desolate?

POLLY [*impishly*]. Well, if any one should *offer*
to see us home or—

TORIES [*in unison, and gaily*]. We all do! We
all do!

POLLY [*with her lowest, most roguish courtesy*].
Then there'll be no refusals on our part.

MR. PRESTON [*delighted*]. Gad! D'ye mean—

[*Laughing and talking in pantomime,
they exeunt,* POLLY *cleverly managing
so that she is last. She gives a
meaning look over her shoulder at*
DAME GREEL. *Immediately the*

[115]

*door at lower left opens cautiously,
and* MR. BRADBURY, *a young patriot of twenty or thereabout, sticks
his head in.*]

MR. BRADBURY. Dame Greel! Hush! Quiet!
The ammunition is moved, and the Committee of
Safety will hold a meeting here without delay.

DAME GREEL [*astonished*]. Heaven bless us!

MR. BRADBURY. It may lose you some of your
Tory trade.

DAME GREEL. Lose it, and welcome!

[*Exit* BRADBURY, *who has not strayed
from door. Instantly* DAME GREEL
*is all animation. She claps her
hands loudly, and the inn boys run
in in answer to her summons, from
right.*]

DAME GREEL. Be brisk with the tables and
chairs! Some gentlemen will soon be here.
[*Table and chairs are put to rights.*] Are you shod
with lead, Nat Tompkins? Bring on that chair,
and quickly! Laggards, laggards, laggards, every
one of you. I can't do my work for seeing that
you do yours. [*She brings pewter tankard and cups
to table.*] Steady with that bowl, Jack. Don't

drop it. [*The boys, all save* TOM, *having finished their tasks, exeunt, right.* DAME GREEL *goes to shake her duster out the front door, carrying her broom with her. As she goes* TOM *attempts to take a drink out of the pewter flagon.* DAME GREEL *turns and sees him, darts after him. There is a brief game of cat and mouse.*] Aha! You thought I would not see you! I'll make you smart for that! [*Holding her broom, she chases him around the table. He hides under it.*] You young villain! [*It is in this position that the Committee of Safety, who now enter from background, find them.*] Beg pardon, sirs. I did not hear you coming. Good day, Mr. Preble. Good day, Mr. Fox. The table is ready, sirs. [*Exeunt* DAME GREEL *and* TOM, *right. Men gather about table.*]

MR. FOX. Friends, men of the Committee of Safety, we are gathered here to decide and to report on the situation in our town.

MR. PREBLE. I am in hopes that the spirit of our American Minute Men will save the country.

MR. FOX. "In hopes!" Good heavens! Give us a regular government or we are undone! [*An* AMERICAN MESSENGER *appears in doorway.*] Here comes one of our messengers. What news?

[*Enter the* AMERICAN MESSENGER.]

AMERICAN MESSENGER [*panting*]. The worst of news! The treacherous Mowatt is in the harbor with three British ships.

MR. MAYO [*looking out the door*]. Here comes a British messenger.

> [MOWATT'S *messenger, carrying a letter and a white flag of truce, appears in doorway, then enters.* MR. PREBLE *meets him, and takes the letter. Reads.*]

MR. PREBLE. "I have orders to execute a just punishment on the town of Falmouth. . . . I warn you to remove without delay. . . . The officer who will deliver this letter I expect to return immediately, unmolested. H. MOWATT."

> [*While the letter has been read* DAME GREEL *and the four inn boys enter cautiously from right, up stage, and stand there motionless, watching all that goes forward.*]

MR. PREBLE. Gentlemen, what do you say? Shall we give in, or shall the war-ship shell the town. What do you say?

MR. FOX. I say, return the letter to Mowatt and say that you defy him.

OMNES [*save* BRITISH MESSENGER]. Aye! Aye! [*The words ring rousingly.*]

BRITISH MESSENGER. One moment. I have Captain Mowatt's orders to say that if you will give him prisoners and all the firearms which the town contains he will spare you. If not, he will open fire at once. Surrender or burn.

MR. PREBLE [*turning*]. Fellow-citizens, you have heard Captain Mowatt's message. What do you say?

MR. BRADBURY. I say that we do not surrender.

MR. MAYO. I say let him burn the town to ashes.

OMNES [*except the* BRITISH MESSENGER]. I say so, too. And I! And I! And I! [*The effect is almost that of a cheer.*]

MR. PREBLE [*to* BRITISH MESSENGER]. You have heard the message, sir. Return and tell Captain Mowatt that our citizens will not surrender.

BRITISH MESSENGER. Then the women must leave the city.

[DAME GREEL *steps forward, her eyes ablaze, her broom in hand.*]

DAME GREEL. That's right for the women with children, but you tell Captain Mowatt from me that I'll stay here in spite of his cannon-balls.

[119]

[MESSENGER *falls back a step, alarmed at her manner. She follows.*] I defy him and the whole British navy!

> [*She brings her broom down with a whack on the* BRITISH MESSENGER. *He has already been given his letter by* MR. PREBLE. *Now he turns and flees for his life. From outside, faint and far, the notes of "Yankee Doodle."* DAME GREEL *drops her broom, and, snatching her bowls and tankard from table, presses them on* MR. BRADBURY. *He asks, "What's this?" amazedly.*]

DAME GREEL. You'll be needing pewter for bullets, if you run short, and you can melt them down. I like to think of my old jugs singing through the air. [*Exeunt the* COMMITTEE OF SAFETY *and the* AMERICAN MESSENGER. *The notes of "Yankee Doodle" grow stronger.*] Move my table, lads! We may need it for a barricade. [*She takes down the musket and powder-horn from above the hearth.*]

TOM [*awed, and staring at her*]. You're not going to use the musket?

DAME GREEL [*slinging the powder-horn to her*

waist and trying the lock of the musket]. Did ye think that dancing was all we women could do? Ha! There's learning coming to you! 'Tis the blood o' Maine that runs in my veins, my lad. And I tell you, though Maine may suffer, she never gives up.

> [*The sound of "Yankee Doodle" mingles with a sudden thunder of musketry as* DAME GREEL *moves through the door in background, shouldering her musket, a light about her face.*]

COSTUMING THE PLAYS

COSTUMING THE PLAYS

This chapter purposes to give an idea of how to costume the following plays simply and effectively. It will deal with them in their order according to the list given in the table of contents.

The *colors* of the costumes in "The Pioneers" are already indicated in the text. Any illustrated history of the United States will give the pictures of Puritan costumes. The material used may be cambric, with the glazed side turned inward. Ordinary low black shoes, with as square toes as possible, and buckles made of cardboard covered with *dull*-silvered paper. Silkoline (or cheese-cloth) will garb The Powers of the Forest and The Powers of the River. See that it hangs in straight Grecian lines and is not bunchy. There should be bloomers and a straight underdress of silkoline wide enough to dance in, and then the overdress. It should be ankle-length, without a hem, and the material should not be cut too evenly. A prim look is not what is wanted.

White stockings and sandals for The Powers of the River. Tan stockings and brown sandals for The Powers of the Forest. On no account should high-heeled slippers be worn. They look ridiculous. Care should be taken to have the foot-gear as nearly alike as possible. The Mist Maidens can wear white cotton crêpe, or silkoline, made in the same manner as described above. All the scarfs should be chiffon. Nothing else floats as delicately or can be whipped into expression as quickly and easily. The Gray and Brown Ones of the Forest wear green and brown cheese-cloth that falls straighter and tighter than the other costumes to give the effect of an animal skin. They wear animal heads with upstanding wolfish ears, tan stockings and sandals. Fever wears scarlet silkoline and foot-gear. Famine wears gray of the same material. Death wears a black tight-fitting suit on which the outline of a skeleton is either painted or basted; a skull mask.

In "The Fountain of Youth" the Spaniards' costumes of silk, velvet, and armor—the former soiled and the latter dull—should be, if possible, hired from a costumer. In towns where a full range of costumes is not kept garments known as a "Captain John Smith" outfit may be substituted for the real thing. Be careful that they are not all alike in color. Other costumes may be copied from Eggleston's *Illustrated History of the United States*. These, of course, are the authentic ones. The Captain John Smith is of a much later period, and should only be used "when all signs fail." An excellent picture of Ponce de Leon will be found in *The History of the United States*, by E. Benjamin Andrews. The Spirit of the Fountain should wear white Grecian robes of cotton crêpe or chiffon. Both hers and the costumes of The Daughters of the Dawn should be made according to the directions for The Powers of the Forest found in "The Pioneers." The Guardian of the Fountain also wears white stockings and silver sandals. The Daughters of the Dawn wear dawn-pink silkoline, both pale and rosy. Their hair is worn unbound. They have white stockings and white sandals.

In "May-Day" the two Puritan maidens wear cambric with the unglazed side worn outward, and square-toed shoes with buckles. Gideon may wear a Puritan costume of either wool or a simulation of wool made by wearing cambric in the same fashion. He has a long cloak. (See pictures in the best illustrated editions of *Pilgrim's Progress*, also in histories of the United States.) The Fool wears the traditional May-day costume, one-half of which is bright blue and the other half bright yellow. His cap jingles with bells, and there are bells placed about his costume. Robin Hood wears Lincoln green. Maid Marian, Lincoln green also. Cambric of the right shade, unglazed side outward, will be found useful for their costumes. For the other costumes good pictures of morris-dancers should be copied.

In "The Vanishing Race" the Indian men wear tan-colored tight-fitting costumes and breech-clouts preferably; but, since civilization had touched their race at that time, the tan-colored trousered Indian suits could be worn if preferred. They could be simply made by stitching tan fringe down the sides of tan trousers such as workmen wear and making a khaki Indian tunic that comes to a little above the knee. It should be fringed a little at the sides and ends and painted on the breast with Indian designs. The Indian wigs may be hired or made of black cheese-cloth braided into war-locks and fastened to a tightly fitting skull-cap. The feathers and head-gear will partly hide the wig. Be sure that the Indians are not guilty of shoes. If not moccasins, have tan canvas tennis-shoes, beaded. The costumes for the Indian women and maidens may also be made of khaki, fringed and beaded. Good ideas for these can be copied from *The Camp-Fire Girl's Book*, which can be had from Doubleday, Page & Co., Garden City, New York. The same idea for foot-gear that the men have. Striking Indian blankets can be made from canton flannel. The costumes of the Dutch settlers can be found in illustrated histories of the United States. They are suggestive of the Puritan costumes. Full knee-breeches, coat (belted like a Norfolk jacket), and collar and cuffs. Also the so-called "pork-pie" hats with a deep brim, made of black felt. Square-toed shoes and buckles. The same long, full riding - cloaks as those of the Puritans. The Dutch were thrifty, as goes without saying, and except on great state occasions did not indulge in silk, velvet, and satin. Woolen homespun was their daily wear. The colors for these pioneers might be, Arent van Curler, forest green; Jan Wemp, dark brown; Van Valsen, dark blue; Van Slyck, dark plum. It is better to hire these costumes at a costumer's. Sawara's costume should be more gorgeously painted than those of any of the other Indian women, and great beads and pieces of burnished shell should be strung about her neck. Her beaded head-dress should be scarlet and silver.

In "The Passing of Hiawatha" the braves and chieftains wear tight-fitting Indian suits and the customary head - gear, breech - clout, beads, and wampum. Be careful that their faces and hands are stained brown. All the young braves and the chieftains wear war-bonnets. For other details of their costume see notes on "The Vanishing Race." For the costumes of the Indian maidens and women see the notes on "The Vanishing Race" also. For directions for making the robes of The Spirits of the Sunset see the directions for costuming The Powers of the River and The Powers of the Forest in "The Pioneers." Their robes are pale pink and deeper pink, like the hues of sunset. They carry pink chiffon scarfs in their dance, which float as they beckon. Their hair is worn flying, and they have white stockings and white sandals.

For "Dame Greel o' Portland Town" colonial costumes are worn. Dame Greel might wear a green overdress and a scarlet petticoat. In this case her dress should be the only one with a hint of scarlet, which is a strong color before which other colors pale. The girls should wear pretty flowered muslins of varying shades of rose, pale blue, pale yellow, and lavender. The patriots (men) should wear grays, browns, blues, and their suits should be, if possible, plainly made and of plain material. They were going about the business of every day, and not to a rout or ball. The Tories may wear clothes that are a trifle finer and suggest fops. They may be in shades of old rose, dull purple, dark green, gray, or black. Remember it was morning in a small harbor town, not a state occasion. The patriots should wear their hair in unpowdered queues, the Tories should wear theirs powdered. The British Messenger wears a full white wig; ditto the American Messenger. Dame Greel and the young ladies wear their hair pompadoured but unpowdered. The British and American Messengers wear full military uniforms. The inn boys wear loose white shirts, black knee-breeches, black stockings, and low black shoes. Too many amateur producers costume their colonial scenes as if all the participants were going to a ball. An indoor scene, with people busy about their household tasks, will, through the mistakes of amateur producers, show its players costumed in peach-colored velvet and flowered brocades, utterly destroying the atmosphere that their costumes were meant to create. For those wishing to give this play at the minimum of expense the young ladies might be clad in colonial dresses made by having an overdress of cretonne looped over a petticoat of muslin or one summer dress looped over another. With these the customary white fichu is worn. The men's costumes, in an emergency, might be made by basting back ordinary dress-coats, and applying gold braid, cretonne cuffs and collars, and white wrist and neck ruffles. Also, of course, they wear knee-breeches. The costumes for the Messengers would undoubtedly have to be hired.

MUSIC

MUSIC

("The Pioneers")

1. "Humoresque." Dvorak.

2. "The Pizzicato Polka," from the "Ballet Sylvia." Leo Delibes.

3. "To a Water-lily," Edward MacDowell; or "Arabesque 2," Debussy.

4. "The Hall of the Mountain King," from the "Peer Gynt" Suite, Grieg; and "The Death of Ase," from the same Suite.

5. "Anitra's Dance," from the "Peer Gynt" Suite. Greig.

6. "Melody in F." Rubinstein.

("The Fountain of Youth")

1. "Spring Song." Mendelssohn.

2. "Idyllo." Theodore Lack.

("May-Day")

English folk-dance music to be found in *Folk Dances*, by Elizabeth Burchenal; *The Folk Dance*

PLAYS OF THE PIONEERS

Book, by C. Ward Crampton; and *The Guild of Play Books*, edited by Curwen, London, England.

("The Vanishing Race")

1. (Dance of Indian maiden.) "The Chattering Squaw." Harvey Worthington Loomis.
2. "From an Indian Lodge." Edward Mac-Dowell.
3. The same.

("The Passing of Hiawatha")

1. "Passamaquoddy Dance Song" and "Music of the Calumet," from "Legends of the Redmen," Harvey Worthington Loomis; also "Prayer to Manitou," Victor Herbert.
2. (For war-dance.) "Apache Indian Scalp Song," John Philip Sousa, from "Airs of All Nations."
3. (For Spirits of the Sunset.) Overture to "Hiawatha's Departure." Coleridge Taylor.

("Dame Greel o' Portland Town")

1. Beethoven's "Minuet in G."
2. "Yankee Doodle."

BIBLIOGRAPHY

BIBLIOGRAPHY

("The Pioneers")

Eggleston's *History of the United States*. (Illustrated.)
The Indian and the Pioneer. Rose N. Yawger.

("The Fountain of Youth")

Eggleston's *History of the United States*. (Illustrated.)
Bancroft's *History of the United States*.
History of the United States. E. Benjamin Andrews. (Illustrated.)

("May-Day")

Eggleston's *History of the United States*. (Illustrated.)
Percival Chubb's *Plays and Festivals*.
Folk Festivals. Mary Needham.
The Festival Book. Jeanette Lincoln.
Folk Dances and Singing Games. Elizabeth Burchenal.

PLAYS OF THE PIONEERS

The Folk Dance Book. C. Ward Crampton.
The Guild of Play Books. Curwen (London).

("The Vanishing Race")

Town Records of Schenectady, New York.
History of Albany County.
Historic New York Towns. Powell.
History of the United States. E. Benjamin Andrews.
The Jesuits in North America. Parkman.
The Last of the Mohicans. Cooper.
The Indian Tribes of the United States. F. S. Drake.
Algic Researches. Schoolcraft.
Proceedings of the American Association for the Advancement of Science (1881).

"(The Passing of Hiawatha")

Hiawatha. Longfellow.
The Story of the Indian. G. B. Grinnell.
Blackfoot Lodge Tales. G. B. Grinnell.
La Salle and the Discovery of the Great West. Parkman.
The Jesuits in North America. Parkman.
The Myth of Hiawatha. Schoolcraft.
Stories from Indian Wigwams and Northern Camp-fires. E. R. Young.

BIBLIOGRAPHY

("Dame Greel o' Portland Town")

Historic Towns of New England.   Lyman Powell.
History of Portland.   William Willis.
Portland.   Neal.
Portland and Vicinity.   Elwell.
Journals of the Rev. Thomas Smith and the Rev. Silas Deane.   Edited by William Willis.

PRODUCING OUTDOOR PAGEANTS
AND PLAYS

PRODUCING OUTDOOR
PAGEANTS AND PLAYS

THREE kinds of outdoor drama are at present growing more and more wide-spread in this country — the pageant, the masque, and the outdoor play. The historical pageant shows in a series of chronological scenes (or episodes, as they are technically called) the life of a given community or city from its first settlement down to the problems of the present day. It may have ten or sixteen scenes, or perhaps only six, and from three hundred to several thousand pageant players and from one thousand to fifty thousand spectators. It must have special music, costumes, properties, and—if it be given at night—special lighting effects. The same holds true of the masque, a form of drama conveying a constructive idea rather than the concrete history of a place. Lastly, there is the outdoor play, familiar from time immemorial. The play may need a "coach," but the pageant and masque need more than a coach—they demand expert leadership, a pageant or masque director who will write the pageant book, co-ordinating spoken speech, pantomime, music, and dancing, and who will afterward direct the pageant players. But as there are many communities, as well as colleges, normal schools, and high schools, not always able, for monetary or other reasons, to avail themselves of such directorship, the pageant-play will give scope for pageant effects on a small scale—a scale which any amateur director may attempt, using one, two, or three pageant-plays according to the conditions that are to be met.

The predominant factor in staging an outdoor play or pageant is the selection of the pageant stage. To this all other conditions are subordinate. In selecting the stage the three most important things to be considered are suitability, accessibility, and picturesqueness. By suitability is meant that the outdoor stage shall be an appropriate setting for the material on hand, that it shall have a good background, entrances, and exits. If the pageant or pageant-play is supposed to be something that will interest not only the community in which it is given, but near-by communities, then it must be within easy distance of car-lines or a road. The stage should be picturesque, or should be made so. Nothing can so mar a performance as an unsuitable stage. Of course a large pageant requires a large stage, while a small pageant may be made to look larger than it really is by means of its background and general stage-setting. This is also true of plays. A medium large stage is required for a play with a large cast, while a play with a small cast should be produced on a smaller and shallower stage in order to get the best effects. This does not mean that the stage should be cramped. It is merely a warning against having the pageant players look too scattered and inadequate—an effect often unconsciously produced by having too deep a stage or too few people on too spreading a surface. Of course in a scene that is to convey a sense of desolation or loneliness a few people appearing on a large stage will give the right effect. But in general it is wise to avoid giving a sense of too few people. A stage that is too large can have trees set in, right, left, and background, which will bring the action within a smaller compass. A large stage is approximately one hundred feet long by fifty feet deep, and a small stage fifty feet long and twenty or thirty feet deep.

The ideal outdoor stage is a level greensward with trees right, left, and background. If possible, there should be no trees on the stage itself, which should be left free for dancing. In front of the stage should be a gradual slope where the audience can sit on the grass or where a grandstand can be erected. But such spots combining all requirements are rare, save in college grounds, and the amateur director must cope with all sorts of problems before an adequate stage can be selected. Acoustics must be reckoned with in selecting a play or pageant site. The orchestra and voices of the players must be considered. The committee choosing such a site must try to see how voices will carry before ultimately deciding. Those who have the play in charge need scarcely be warned against selecting a spot with an echo, or a place where the clang of street-cars or trains is apt to drown the voices of the players. A lake or bay for a background vista is lovely to look at, but makes things very difficult for an orchestra unless a sounding-board can be provided. Even then an augmented orchestra must be used, or a band will be found to give the most satisfaction. The sun is also a factor to be reckoned with. It is perhaps more difficult to have the audience sit facing it than to have the players face it, since they can shift their positions, and the audience cannot. To have the stage face north or south is best.

In regard to seats: there are many parks and

athletic fields where grand - stands have already been erected and are ready and waiting for an audience. But the stage in front of them is usually flat and treeless and devoid of grass. The thing to be done in this case is to map out the size the stage is to be and then put (pine) trees in the background and at right and left sides. A quantity of newly cut grass, kept dampened till the last moment, can be strewn flatly over the stage before the performance begins. This will take away from the arid look. If enough trees cannot be had, or if there are no trees, *forest screens* can be constructed. These are made by having posts some six feet high run into the ground and meshed "chicken-wire" fastened to them. Into this chicken-wire should be woven tree-branches, vines, green festoons—anything that will make a good screen. As to the placing of the screens— there should be two at the right of the stage, two at the left, and a long one across background. Slight spaces between them will leave room for exits and entrances. Nothing so destroys the illusion of a play or pageant as to see the characters who are to take part in it loitering on the edges of the stage before it is their turn to appear. Therefore, if the forest screens mask the stage but do not sufficiently hide the players once they have left the scene, construct two more, thus:

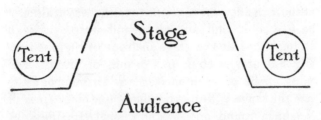

These screens are valuable not only in themselves, but in the way they can be used to augment effects. They make a sparse background of trees look denser, they are invaluable for making a shallow stage *suggest* depth, and they are an admirable foil for costumes, showing up color effects wonderfully well. In places where acoustics are bad they act as a sounding-board. They can be used to hide blots on the landscape. They can even suggest a primeval forest. It should be remembered that a background of trees, real or artificial, accomplishes the same purpose as a backdrop in a theater. A word should be said here about the posts to which the wire is fastened. They must, of course, be painted brown or green or wrapped with brown burlap. If the dressing-room tents are near the stage, and their white or khaki canvas intrudes on the eye of the audience, a forest screen will again be found useful, and the top of the tents can be loosely covered with green boughs or leaves. This has been done in several pageants.

OUTDOOR PAGEANTS AND PLAYS

In a prairie town where not even trees could be had as background the director used the wire screens, and an hour or so before the performance began they were covered with dark-green unglazed muslin over which were fastened festoons of Dennison's tissue-paper garlands.

Forest screens made with actual tree-branches not only make glad the waste places but can be used effectively on the lawns of private estates and country clubs for small masques and pageants.

If an outdoor play with a scene suggesting a forest is given in a spot where unsightly buildings intrude, have tall, slender poles, wound with green, and have ropes of evergreen and strips of dark-green bunting strung between them. (For these poles fishing-rods covered in green are not a bad device, but they must be firmly placed.)

As is well known, the rehearsals of an outdoor play or pageant should take place in a hall or large room that has a good floor for dancing before they are taken into the open. The dances should be rehearsed separately from the play, dancers and players to come together for the first time only when the rehearsals are well under way. Those who are attempting outdoor dramatics for the first time will find it a great aid to both player and director to go to the outdoor stage at the second or third rehearsal when the play is still in the rough and get an idea of stage proportions, exits, entrances, grouping, that can be kept clearly in mind while further rehearsals are going on indoors. *Too great stress cannot be laid on the value of this.* The dance-director and those who are to dance on the outdoor stage should have this early opportunity of approximating how many bars of music it will take to bring them to the part of the stage on which their dance is to begin. They will know whether the introduction needs to be repeated or not, for, unless otherwise stated, the music is supposed to begin before they enter to build up the atmosphere of their scene.

Of course the indoor rehearsals will be entirely with piano, or piano and violin, but if possible there should be a rehearsal with orchestra for the dancers alone before the full-dress rehearsal with orchestra. While rehearsing it should be kept in mind that an outdoor play, far more than an indoor play, must, in case any of the words are lost, make a series of telling pictures, must constantly appeal to the eye. This quality is obtained not merely through care in the grouping of the principals, but through the action of the supernumeraries. See that the latter are well grouped, that they form a still background where such a background is needed, or that they are vibrant and mirror passing emotions when such emotions need to be emphasized. The supernumeraries stand in the same relation to simple outdoor drama as that of the Greek chorus to the old Greek drama, repeating and accenting through pose and gesture pity, rage, curiosity, grief, interest, and a hundred other feelings. This is particularly true of symbolic scenes that depend so largely for their effect on their supernumerary grouping. There is nothing like a long mirror as an aid to amateurs in helping them see the effects to be gained. If the neophyte dryads, spirits, or votive maidens will rehearse individually before a mirror when they are alone it will help them to see their mistakes at once and guide them toward the right way of doing group work.

A word should be said here about having *enough* supernumeraries. If possible the amateur director should see that there are large groups of Mist Maidens, Powers of the River, or whatever other symbolic figures are needed. Twenty Mist Maidens and twenty River Maidens will be just enough for a small stage, but this number can be run up to thirty or forty with an increasingly good effect. Always enlist the services of fifty per cent. more supernumeraries than are needed. There are always unforeseen reasons that will cause people to drop out, and it is well to have others ready to fill their places. If the groups of adults are not large numerically add children to the list as little Water Sprites or Daughters of the Dawn, costuming them exactly like the other dancers. They will help to fill in the group and add to its charm.

There should be a rule, rigidly enforced, that on the hour of the performance none of the players shall be seen unless it is time for them to appear. Many amateurs have an annoying habit of coming to the edge of the "forest" which encircles the outdoor stage and from that vantage-point they peep through and watch the progress of their fellow-players before it is time for their own cues. They are often perfectly visible to the audience and very disconcerting to those who are on the stage. Even if they cannot be clearly seen by the audience, glints of bright color, the flutter of a veil or feather through the trees draws attention to a spot where it was not meant to be drawn. People say, "Oh, little things like this don't count!" But little things like this *do* count. It is often just this attention to little things, to small details, that marks the difference between amateur and professional productions.

Rehearsals should be compassed within a month. A longer time is apt to dull the first sharp edge of interest and lessen enthusiasm. A month's time is here taken to mean diligent, not sporadic, rehearsing.

OUTDOOR PAGEANTS AND PLAYS

It should be borne in mind that the outdoor play needs broader, more simple effects than does the indoor stage. Gestures and tones that would be exaggerations indoors are exactly right out of doors. Big, sweeping, rhythmic effects should be striven for, especially in the dances. The greater scope and freedom for them the better.

On the day of performance the orchestra must be placed where it will not mar the spectators' view of the stage, though it is essential that the orchestra-leader should have the stage in view. At the right or left of the stage is a good place for it. Unless the orchestra chairs are in the shade a background and roof of green boughs (the forest screen again) should be placed for them. If the orchestra is small — that is, if it consists of a piano and a few stringed instruments, an excellent scheme is to have the piano put on a big truck —about the size of a furniture truck—and use this truck as an orchestra platform, with light chairs for the players. The same use can also be made of a wagon in country districts. Drape the truck with dark-green or gaily striped bunting. In this way a piano does not have to be moved up and down, and if more than one performance of the play is given this orchestra truck can easily be driven to and from the grounds. This is a labor-saving device that has often been used with great success.

The director of the orchestra and the director of the dances should have a series of thoroughly understood silent cues that will signal when the dance music is to begin. It may be the waving of a dancer's scarf as she steps forward or the mere entrance of a character to the edge of the stage, but, whatever it is, it must be clearly agreed upon and rehearsed beforehand, and it must not be too obvious to the audience.

A word should be said here about the lighting of an outdoor drama given in the evening. Night, with its mysterious gleams and shadows, with its brightly lighted spaces and spaces blotted with darkness, lends added enchantment to any play. Silvery light and black velvety shadows have a way of mitigating defects and softening crudities. The reason why it is easy to give an outdoor play near the house of some country estate or club is that electric wires can easily and inexpensively be extended and a small switchboard set up near the stage. This is the ideal way of lighting the outdoor stage. Rude logs placed along the front of the stage where the footlights would naturally be, with electric lights fastened to them, make a good set of outdoor footlights, throwing a strong gleam on the stage and yet having their mechanics hidden from the audience. Still another scheme of lighting was tried in the Pageant of Schenectady.

OUTDOOR PAGEANTS AND PLAYS

The pageant stage had a background of woods and a clear foreground. Six tall, slender poles with clusters of lights crowning them were placed where footlights would usually be. The poles, not being as large as the usual pillar, and being quite far apart, did not interfere with a view of the stage, and yet gave the audience light enough by which to find their seats. Thus the light, coming from above, shed a faint white glow like moonlight across the stage. Other lighting was done from the back by means of globes of light, placed at right and left, facing toward background, and so arranged that they sent a point of light back into the forest. On each side of this point of light was entire darkness from which the characters appeared or disappeared. Farther back in the wood, where their lights could not be seen, were the tent dressing-rooms. Between dressing-rooms and the place where the characters made their entrance was a narrow strip of less-lighted ground that seemed dark to the audience but was perfectly clear to the players. Care was taken that there were no loiterers fringing the path of light. The place was for the time being a primeval forest, moonlit and flecked with shadow, while in the palely lighted foreground gleamed the crimson of the camp-fire.

Where electric lighting cannot be had two engine headlights set facing the stage have been made to do excellent service. Failing even these, the aforementioned logs, placed where the footlights are to be, and candles set in them, with sockets and glass shades, may be made to do instead of electric lights. Lamps are apt to smoke and smell, and lanterns are too dim, hence the suggestion of candles. The log should be thoroughly dampened for fear of any accident resulting from breeze and flame.

In arranging the committee side of the play have a chairman of costumes, of properties, of music, of the outdoor stage, and of printing—which should include the printing of programs. There should also be a secretary and treasurer.

The costumes should, if possible, be mostly home-made. They will have better line and color than those obtained at a costumer's. The initial expense will not be very much greater—may even be very much less. Moreover, the costumes will remain the property of their owners, or the community at large, and not one but many plays may be given with them. The costumes from all pageants and plays should be saved for future efforts. Indeed one of the best things in connection with the nation-wide renaissance of the pageant, masque, and play is the fact that in all such performances the people of the community

OUTDOOR PAGEANTS AND PLAYS

are taking some of the arts of the theater into their own hands. The players, dancers, musicians, and costume artists are recruited from the community just as they were in the glowing medieval days of the guild workers. And, let us hope, with the same results!

THE END